THE
GIRL'S BOOK
OF
ENCHANTMENTS

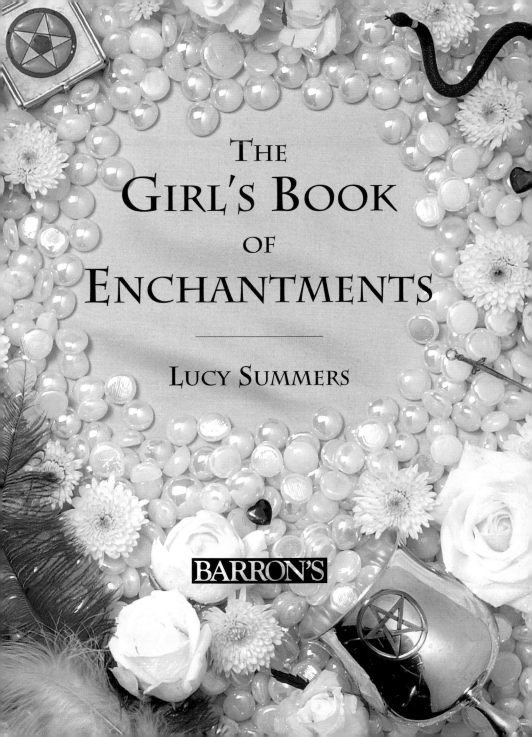

THE
GIRL'S BOOK
OF
ENCHANTMENTS

LUCY SUMMERS

BARRON'S

A QUARTO BOOK

First edition for the United States, its territories
and dependencies, and Canada published in
2002 by Barron's Educational Series, Inc.

All inquiries should be addressed to:
Barron's Educational Series, Inc.
250 Wireless Boulevard
Hauppauge, New York 11788
http://www.barronseduc.com

International Standard Book No. 0-7641-5522-9

Library of Congress Catalog Card No.
2001097561

QUAR.TBE

Conceived, designed, and produced by
Quarto Publishing plc
The Old Brewery
6 Blundell Street
London N7 9BH

Project Editor Tracie Lee Davis
Senior Art Editor Sally Bond
Assistant Art Director Penny Cobb
Designer and Illustrator Trevor Newman
Editor Andy Armitage
Photographer Colin Bowling
Proofreader Anne Plume
Indexer Pamela Ellis

Art Director Moira Clinch
Publisher Piers Spence

Manufactured by Universal Graphics
Pte Ltd., Singapore
Printed by Midas Printing
International Ltd., China

9 8 7 6 5 4 3 2 1

NOTE
The author, publisher, and copyright holder
assume no responsibility for any injury or
damage caused or sustained while using the
recipes and rituals described in this book.

CONTENTS

Let the Sourcery Commence   6
Essential Ingredients   8
Unlocking Hidden Powers   10
Elemental Lore   14

HEX AND THE CITY   16

Easy Assignments   20
Forever Friends   22
Computer Charmer   24
City Oasis   26
In With the In-crowd   28
Smog Buster   30
Urban Warrior   32

THE ART OF RICHCRAFT   34

Top of the Class   38
Merlin's Gold   40
Money Spinner   42
Shop Till You Drop   44
Perfect Saturday Job Spell   46
Luck, be a Lady   48
Career Chooser   50
Tried and Tested   52

LOVE AND SCENTUALITY 54

Kiss Me Quick 58
Love Starter 60
Love Fizzler 62
Relationship Booster 64
I Want You Back 66
To Heal a Broken Heart 68
Fidelity Knot 70

BEAUTY AND BODY 72

My Body, My Temple 76
Face Magic 78
Spot Be Gone 80
Crowning Glory 82
Cleopatra's Oil 84
Mirror, Mirror 86
Bright Eyes 88

SPIRIT POWER 90

Meet Your Spirit Guide 94
Magical Mini Herb Garden 96
Faery Shake 98
Psychic Scrying Bowl 100
Ghostbuster 102
Hudu Doll 104
Healing Crystal Spell 106

BEWITCHING SEASONS 108

Oracle of Spring 112
Summer Worship 114
Eternal Energy (Sealed Spell) 116
Fall Magic 118
Soul-mate Charm (Sealed Spell) 120
Winter Weaving 122
Ultimate Banisher 124
(Sealed Spell)

Index 126
Credits 128

LET THE SORCERY COMMENCE

Spellcasting is an art as ancient as mankind. The shamans of prehistory practiced magic to bring good hunts and to cure illness among the tribe. These attempts to influence the outcome of events by magical means continued through the centuries, in every land, in one form or another. Today, magical rituals are still practiced by indigenous tribes as well as followers of neopagan groups. Indeed, the art of spellcraft is as relevant today as it was in the Stone Age. We still have difficulties and situations that need a resolution, although admittedly the types of problems may have changed.

BELOW Spellcraft can be practiced by anyone as long as they approach it with an open mind.

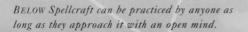

Making Magic

So what is magic, and do you have to become an initiated witch or wizard to practice it? Magic is within us and all around us. All we have to do to harness its powers is to learn a

few tricks. Anyone can do this. Yes, witches and wizards do practice spellcraft, but you do not have to become one to learn the basics. The simple spells detailed in this book do not use long and complicated rituals. Instead, they use easy-to-find ingredients and props that focus the will onto what is required.

These spells are designed to bring about positive changes in your life. There are no spells in this book that will cause another harm. To set about magic with a bad purpose in mind would be highly unethical and, as the old lore goes, such a spell would rebound upon the caster by the power of three. Negative magic twists the user and generally turns him or her into someone who is not a very nice person with not a very nice life. On the other hand, positive magic can only enhance both you and your environment, bringing you the success, friendships, romances, and jobs that you wish for. When performed with a good heart, a small dose of humor, and a heap of sincerity, magic does work—so be careful what you ask for!

ABOVE People of other cultures, such as these Huichol Indians, also include magic and ritual in their daily lives

ESSENTIAL INGREDIENTS

Traditional witchcraft uses a whole range of tools and ingredients that must be either bought or made, and then ritually consecrated. However, for the purpose of simple spellcraft you need to obtain and do much less. Here are a few of the more necessary items.

An altar

An altar is useful to have for some if not all spells. It can be simply made by using an old wooden box, tea chest, or table, just as long as it is stable enough not to wobble when lit candles are placed upon it. To make it look more magical, drape it with an altar cloth. Green or white are good colors, although you can always match the color to the spell you are performing.

Altars can also be used when not casting a spell as a meditation focus, or a place where you can honor the passing seasons with various flowers, nuts, blossoms, or pebbles.

Candles

Candles are a great aid to focus and also in increasing the energy available to a spell. The colors have different correspondences.

COLOR/SPELL ENERGY

Yellow/gold • *Strength, abundance, happiness*

White/silver/violet • *Purity, psychic work, healing*

Red • *Protection, vitality, lust*

Orange • *Communication, mental work, career*

Blue • *Healing, wealth*

Green or pink • *Love, romance, friendship, harmony*

Black • *Banishing, getting rid of negative thoughts*

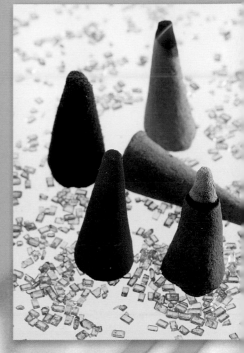

ABOVE Incense cones.

Incense

Like candles, incense adds the right magical atmosphere as well as helping to send your wishes out to the cosmos. Unless otherwise stated, use whatever incense you feel most magical with.

Other ingredients

Spells often use other natural ingredients, such as plants, stones, crystals, or feathers, all of which are imbued with their own particular energy. Bear in mind when collecting fresh plant material that you should always do it with respect. Ask the plant for its permission first and tell it your purpose. Then, after you have removed what you need (and only what you need), leave a small offering as a means of thanks. This can be either a pinch of tobacco or a piece of your own hair.

UNLOCKING HIDDEN POWERS

How do we weave magic?

The energy responsible for magic lies all around us as well as within us. It is an unseen current, rather like electricity or electromagnetism, except that it connects everyone and everything in the universe. When we focus our will on what we want to happen, quite often this is enough to influence the energy to create the necessary changes and events that will allow the goal to materialize.

Using the will

Using your will for magic means that you will need to develop and practice one vital skill: the art of visualization. You will need to be able to imagine your desired outcomes and keep them vividly in your head. You can practice this technique by placing a solid object in front of you—for example, an apple. Observe it for a minute, then close your eyes and recall every detail in your imagination. Don't just "see" it. You must also be able to "feel," "taste," "smell," and "hear" it.

LEFT Many common household items can be used in spells.

The rules of spellcasting

It is a definite no-no to use magic to harm others. Spells used in this way often come back upon the spellcaster, so don't try it, no matter how angry you are. Spells also tend to work on the principle that you get what you need rather than what you want. For instance, a money spell will probably bring you only enough to tide you over in troubled times rather a million dollars.

Before casting any spell, think it out first. Are you doing it on an impulse you may regret later? After all, magic can produce great changes in your life, so use it only if you are sincere about what you want. Finally, once your spell has outlived its purpose, destroy it. The best way is by burning the ingredients.

RIGHT Magic should create balance and harmony in your life.

Moon magic

Just as the moon influences the tides of the sea, so it also influences the tides of magic. The phases of the moon are important in most magic spells, as moonlight vibes can be powerful allies. Many ancient cultures as well as most modern pagans and witches believe that the moon represents the goddess in her role as Queen of Heaven. In this aspect she brings creativity, inspiration, magic, and knowledge of the cycles of life. When you perform a ritual or ceremony, take into account what phase the moon is in:

 New moon • New beginnings or ideas; the start of a project

 Waxing moon • Spells for positive outcomes, or something gained

 Full moon • The time of completion or fulfillment; psychic work

 Waning moon • Banishing negativity; endings; loss

Sun magic

The sun, too, has a powerful energy and controls the seasons and night and day. Although times of the year and days of the week do not seem to be used in modern magic as much as the moon, they are included here in case you wish to add them:

Spring • beginnings, friendship and courtship; financial gain

Summer • Celebration, marriage, children, fulfillment, love, healing, and happiness

ABOVE *The ancients believed that cosmic forces had an influence on magic and their lives.*

Fall • *Reflection, gathering in, meditative magic*

Winter • *Clearing out unwanted vibes and habits; dream magic*

Days of the week

Astrologers have long assigned the days of the week to the influence of the planets in our solar system. So, if possible, try to arrange for your spellcasting to be on the right day. Then you can be sure that planetary energies will give your spell a cosmic boost.

Sunday • *Sun—courage and strength; vitality; good health; happiness; abundance; protection*

Monday • *Moon—healing; psychic powers; spells involving water; inspiration; creativity*

Tuesday • *Mars—strong protection; energy and fitness; lust; disputes*

Wednesday • *Mercury—communication; examinations; travel; meetings; creativity*

Thursday • *Jupiter—abundance; luck; good health; happiness*

Friday • *Venus—love; friendship; comfort; reconciliation*

Saturday • *Saturn—getting rid of negativity; wisdom*

ELEMENTAL LORE

The elements

Ancient wisdom tells us that the elements are representative of the energies in the environment around us. All aspects of magic either consciously or subconsciously use these forces. For example, whenever we light a candle, we are working with the energy of fire. Incense brings to a spell the energy of air. Therefore, having a basic knowledge of elemental working is important in spellcraft.

Earth

This element symbolizes stability and security. It can be represented by soil, sand, rocks and pebbles, and plants. It is also represented by the witch's symbol of the pentagram. Earth energy is useful in money spells, and spells to protect the environment. Its direction is north.

Air

Air carries ideas, inspirations, and news.
Bring air into your spells by lighting incense
or performing your ritual on a hilltop. Trees
also carry the element of air. Air energy
is useful for getting your wishes heard
and for clearing the mind. Its
direction is east.

Fire

The heat of fire brings
energy, power, and passion
to magic. Used extensively
in candle magic, the flame
of fire can add much to
most spells. However, use
with respect and care—
fire is a volatile energy
that can help you, but
it can also harm. Its
direction is south.

Water

Water cleanses and heals as well
as being representative of the
emotions. To bring water energy to
your spell, place a bowl of it on your
altar. Water is good for psychic work,
love, purification, and healing. Its
direction is west.

LEFT *The four elements of earth, air, fire,
and water make up the magical world we live in.*

Hex
and the
City

FOR THE GIRL ABOUT TOWN

LEFT In the 16th century religious intolerance led to witches being burned at the stake.

THE ART OF WITCHCRAFT ORIGINATED LONG AGO, BUT HAS ALWAYS MANAGED TO KEEP UP WITH THE TIMES, USING WHATEVER IMPLEMENTS AND MATERIALS WERE AVAILABLE. THE WORLD OF TODAY IS NO EXCEPTION. THE DIFFICULTIES MAY HAVE CHANGED—FOR EXAMPLE, COMPUTER GLITCHES WERE NOT A PROBLEM HUNDREDS OF YEARS AGO—BUT THE NEED TO FIND MAGICAL SOLUTIONS HAS NOT.

In the past, witches and spellcasters were often persecuted unto death for their practices. Today, although death is unlikely, people who openly profess to deal in magic may still be subject to ridicule. Therefore, it is still better to keep your art secret from those around you. For some spells, such as Forever Friends or the

Computer Charmer, this may require some ingenuity. But don't worry: These challenges all add to the fun of the moment. The same applies to getting to know your environment. Different places may have different plants or trees growing. Get to know them—not only by looking them up but also by talking silently to them and "sensing" their energy. Once you have built up your own ingredient portfolio from your surroundings, you should be able to conjure some spells of your own. Be warned, though, against using poisonous substances— you don't want your magic to land you in the hospital.

Ingredients for city magic needn't include only items that sound old or mysterious. For example, Forever Friends uses an envelope and a ribbon. I'm sure that magical uses could just as easily be devised for the use of paper clips and correction fluid! So, whether you are stuck with schoolwork, need to de-stress, or need to feel safe when you go out downtown, go right ahead and practice some city magic.

BELOW Be aware of the environment around you and learn as much about it as you can.

EASY ASSIGNMENTS

Increase your mental prowess with ancient herb craft

THERE ARE TIMES WHEN THE TASK IN FRONT OF YOU SEEMS HARDER TO CLIMB THAN A MOUNTAIN. ASSIGNMENTS AND OTHER HOMEWORK ALWAYS SEEM TO APPEAR WHEN YOU LEAST NEED THEM—WHEN YOU ARE TIRED OR ARE ALREADY ON A DEADLINE FOR ANOTHER IMPORTANT PROJECT.

This simple piece of herb craft uses ancient plant wisdom to help increase your mental powers and alertness. With this on your side, your homework will be done before you know it!

Place the sage, basil, dill seeds, and coffee into the mortar and grind them to a fine powder with the pestle. When you are happy with the way they look and feel, add the sand and mix well. Place the whole mixture in a jar with a tight-fitting lid so that you will always have some available when you need it.

For your current needs, take a teaspoonful and put it on a plate. From this amount, take a pinch of the mixture and place it somewhere separate. This smaller amount is then mixed with a tiny bit of water until it becomes a paste.

Make sure you don't make it too runny. Then, with your forefinger, paint a little bit of the paste onto the middle of your forehead, between your eyebrows. Gently sprinkle the rest of the dry mixture over your homework. Say:

Magical mixture of plant and sand
Give my work a helping hand
Grant my mind the power to see
Answers to the question that lies before me.

Both brain and paper are marked by this spell
There's no excuse for me not to do well.
And so I shall begin my wisdom's quest
Knowing my work shall be the best.

Sit quietly for a minute or two, aligning your consciousness to the task in front of you. Then gently take the paper in front of you, being careful not to spill any of the magic mixture. Take it outside and shake it out thoughtfully on the ground, saying a silent prayer of thanks to the powers that be for the help you are about to receive.

TAKE ...

YOUR ASSIGNMENT

SAND

PESTLE AND MORTAR

DRIED SAGE

DRIED BASIL

DILL SEEDS

GROUND COFFEE

A LITTLE BIT OF WATER

FOREVER FRIENDS

Banish bad vibes between friends

EVEN THE BEST OF FRIENDS SOMETIMES FALL OUT.
THIS IS BAD ENOUGH WHEN JUST TWO PEOPLE ARE
INVOLVED, BUT IF A WHOLE GROUP BECOMES
AFFECTED BY AN ARGUMENT, THE ATMOSPHERE
CAN BECOME UNBEARABLE. WORDS ARE EASILY
SAID BUT NOT SO EASILY TAKEN BACK.

This spell is designed to calm the air and encourage a
move toward reconciliation and repair. Soon you will all
have forgotten what the argument was about in the first place!
To banish backstabbing and get rid of gossip, try
the following steps:
Under some pretext, get everyone
involved to provide you with a piece of
paper with a sample of their handwriting
on it. Collect these and take them home,
taking care not to mix them with any
other piece of written work.
Then, on a Friday, the day of
Venus, goddess of love and
harmony, take the pieces
of paper and bind them
together with the
pink ribbon, saying:

*I bind you together in friendship. Let all
malice and ill feeling be henceforth banished
from this group. Instead may there be
happiness and harmony, peace, and
compassion within our hearts. As I do will,
so mote it be.*

The above should be said three times in all and then the bound papers should be placed in the envelope and sealed. Place the envelope somewhere safe where it won't be discovered. The bad vibes between you and your friends should soon sort themselves out and you will all be back to having a good time again. By the way, it is best not to show the envelope to your friends. Besides weakening the magic, you will be in danger of becoming known as the group weirdo!

TAKE ...

A SAMPLE OF WRITING FROM EVERYONE IN YOUR GROUP

A PIECE OF PINK RIBBON

AN ENVELOPE, PREFERABLY PINK, BUT WHITE WILL DO

COMPUTER CHARMER

Unravel the mysteries of your computer—by being nice to it!

SOMETIMES IT SEEMS AS IF COMPUTERS HAVE TAKEN OVER THE WORLD. MOST PLACES OF WORK ARE NOW COMPUTERIZED AND MANY HOMES ALSO HAVE ONE OR MORE COMPUTERS. BUT NOT EVERYONE UNDERSTANDS THEM FROM THE INSIDE TO THE OUTSIDE. INDEED, THESE MACHINES STILL MAINTAIN A CERTAIN AURA OF TECHNICAL MYSTERY AND ARE OFTEN ACCUSED OF HAVING A MIND OF THEIR OWN!

It sometimes seems that computers go wrong at the most inopportune moments, causing frustration and a great desire to throw them out of the window and revert to pen and paper. However, help is at hand. Perform the following spell and make your computer your friend.

First of all, treat your computer as if it were indeed your friend. This does not mean that you have to take it out to lunch, but it does mean giving it a good dusting and untangling any tangled cables. Then, select a word processing program and type the following charm:

Bits and bytes, ROM and RAM,
By the mystery of the Motherboard,
I ask you to help me in my work;
Spirit of this computer,
Through silicon chip and processor,

By MS-DOS
and applications,
Within your most
sacred registry,
So you are conjured
To do my will
And cause no ill
To be my aid, my helper,
my friend
Until my work is at an end.

Save and store this in a special place on your computer—make sure no one else will find it! The spell will then stay attached to its memory and will be activated whenever the system is switched on. Remember to talk to your computer (nicely) and keep it clean and in good condition at all times. It may even help to give it a pet name.

TAKE ...

A DUSTER

A QUARTZ CRYSTAL

YOUR COMPUTER

CITY OASIS

A charm to calm before an important test or event

LIFE IN THE CITY, OR EVEN IN A TOWN, CAN SOMETIMES BE VERY HECTIC, LEAVING NO TIME FOR VITAL REST AND RELAXATION. USE THIS TECHNIQUE BEFORE A BIG EVENT OR AFTER A BUSY DAY AT SCHOOL TO CREATE YOUR OWN OASIS OF CALM.

Find yourself a place where you won't be disturbed. Put a drop of lavender oil on your finger and rub it into your temples. Sit with your eyes closed, in a relaxed position, and begin to imagine that your body is getting lighter and lighter. Visualize yourself floating upward, as insubstantial as a feather or a speck of dust. As you rise higher, effortlessly floating through any ceiling or roof, feel yourself rising high above the building, higher and higher until the whole city is spread out beneath you. However, up here you are removed from all the bother and stress. Up here there is nothing to worry about.

A little wispy cloud comes along. You step onto it and sit down. It supports your weight and is soft and comfortable. The cloud takes you higher still, until you are beneath a beautiful arching rainbow. As you sit beneath this rainbow, it begins to shower you with drops of all its colors. Before long you are bathed in a gentle warm radiant rainbow mist. Its subtle energy surrounds you with a feeling of calm and a knowledge that all will be well. After a few minutes, the rainbow fades and the cloud gradually disperses. Slowly

you float back to earth, gently
slipping back through the roof
and ceiling and back again
into your body. Take a few
minutes to orientate yourself
back in the material world,
open your eyes, give a big
smile, and say, "All is well
and I am rested."

TAKE ...

*ESSENTIAL OIL
OF LAVENDER*

IN WITH THE IN-CROWD

Find the confidence to meet new people

SOMETIMES IT CAN BE HARD TO GET UP THE COURAGE TO JOIN A PARTICULAR SOCIAL GROUP. THIS SPELL WILL ENHANCE YOUR CHANCES AT JOINING IN. ANY SHYNESS YOU HAVE SHOULD DISAPPEAR AND YOU WILL BECOME ONE OF THOSE ADMIRED AND ENVIED BY OTHERS FOR THE CIRCLES YOU MOVE IN.

On an evening near to the full moon, take the blue pieces of wool. Tie a knot in the ends of the first piece so that it forms a circle. Loop the next piece of wool within the first so that it forms the beginning of a chain. Do the same with all the rest of the blue pieces until you have a line of linked circles. As you do this, say:

Circles within circles, loops within groups
I wish to be in the company of (name of individuals or club)
By all the stars in the sky
By all the grains of sand on the beach
I choose these as my friends, my tribe, my clan
May they hear my call
And welcome me within their ranks
So mote it be.

At this point, visualize yourself being warmly welcomed by your new friends or the people in your club. When the picture is strong enough, take the piece of white wool and use it to join the beginning and end of the blue wool links so that a complete circle is formed. Say:

I shall be the newest link in the circle
I shall bind it all together
I shall be valued for what I can bring
I shall be part of these friends
For as long as I do wish.

Place the candle in a steady holder and place the circle of wool around the base. Light the candle while chanting:

Fire add energy to this charm
And from it let there be no harm
May this spell work well for me
As I do will, so mote it be!

Leave the candle burning for an hour before snuffing it out. Put the charm in a safe place and do not disturb it for at least a month.

TAKE ...

SEVERAL PIECES OF BLUE WOOL ABOUT 3 INCHES (6CM) LONG

A PIECE OF WHITE WOOL ABOUT 3 INCHES (6CM) LONG

A BLUE CANDLE

SMOG BUSTER

Cope with smoky environments and city smog

TODAY'S WORLD IS A HEAVILY POLLUTED ONE, WITH THE AIR WE BREATHE BEING ESPECIALLY FULL OF FUMES. POLLUTION ALSO ATTRACTS DIRT OF A DIFFERENT KIND, THAT OF NEGATIVE ENERGIES. THESE ENERGIES ARE TOTALLY AT HOME WITH SUBSTANCES THAT CAUSE BOTH US AND OUR PLANET TO GET ILL.

When we get home after a day in the city or any other heavily polluted environment, we can feel so dirty, both inside and out.

Water and salt are cleansing, protective, and healing, as is rosemary. To perform this spell, take the rosemary and place it into the infuser ball. Put the ball in a jar or cup, boil some water, and pour a cupful over the herb. Allow this to infuse for five minutes. While it is infusing, add a pinch of salt and hold your hands over the liquid. Visualize a silver-blue light streaming from the palms of your hands and entering the infusion. Say:

Salt and water and holy herb, I do bless you with the power of light that you may ward off all malignancy where you are cast. As I do will, so mote it be.

TAKE ...

*A SMALL, PUMP-TYPE,
AEROSOL PERFUME BOTTLE*

*A TEASPOONFUL OF
ROSEMARY (DRIED OR
FRESH AND CRUSHED)*

WATER

AN INFUSER BALL

A PINCH OF SALT

When the mixture has cooled, pour it into
the perfume bottle. It is now ready and
portable for you to take anywhere. To use
it at school, for example, spray the liquid in
a circle around you, while saying (under your
breath if you have to):

*Salt and water and holy herb,
do your work:
Around me no dark smog shall lurk.*

Remember, the mixture will need to
be replaced every three or four days, and
crystallized salt may need to be rinsed from
the pump spray mechanism.

URBAN WARRIOR

Awaken your inner warrior for safe traveling and strength

WARRIORS OF LONG AGO OFTEN WORE FACE PAINT BOTH AS A SYMBOL OF DIVINE PROTECTION AND ALSO TO SCARE THE ENEMY. HOW DO YOU THINK YOUR OWN FACE WOULD LOOK? YOU CAN HAVE SOME FUN AND PROTECT YOURSELF AT THE SAME TIME!

Think about how you would paint your face and then make a quick sketch of it on the piece of paper. Don't be afraid to experiment and try out different combinations; perhaps you would put a streak of red from forehead to chin, or maybe a band of black across your eyes. If you wish, you could even try it out on your face using face paints. When you are sure of your own individual warrior marks, make a final drawing and put it safely away so that you can always find it if you need to remind yourself.

This next part is to be done just before you go out, especially if you feel in need of extra protection. Stand in front of a mirror and stand up straight. With your fingers, draw your imaginary warrior marks on your face. They may be invisible to others, but you will know they are there. Visualize a glowing, oval-shaped light surrounding your whole body. This is your aura.

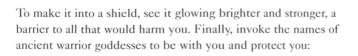

To make it into a shield, see it glowing brighter and stronger, a barrier to all that would harm you. Finally, invoke the names of ancient warrior goddesses to be with you and protect you:

Inanna, Lady of Sumer, Queen of Heaven, be in front of me.
Athena, protectress of Athens, be behind me.
Sekhmet, fiery defender of Egypt, be to the left of me.
Scathach, trainer of warriors, be to the right of me.
Morrigan, Celtic goddess of battle, be below me.
Artemis, with your skilled aim, be above me.
Goddess power all around me
That no harm shall befall me this night—
So mote it be.

TAKE ...

SOME PAPER

COLORED PENS OR PENCILS

THE ART OF
RICHCRAFT

MONEY MAKES THE WORLD GO ROUND

USING MAGICAL SPELLS TO GAIN MONEY HAS ALWAYS
ATTRACTED POTENTIAL ENCHANTERS TO THE ART.
HOWEVER, IT MUST BE SAID THAT YOU DON'T SEE MANY
MILLIONAIRES IN THE WITCHING WORLD. SO WHY IS THIS?
SURELY, HAVING THE WONDERFUL POWER OF THE COSMOS
AT YOUR COMMAND SHOULD BE ENOUGH TO BRING IN THE
GOODIES, SHOULDN'T IT?

Well, I'm sorry to say that it isn't as simple as that. As has been stated
elsewhere, magic has its peculiar little rules, one of them being that you tend
to get only what you need. And, since most of us don't actually need a million
dollars (although it would be rather nice), it doesn't come our way.

That being said, magical means can still be used to influence the universe to
bring luck and abundance into your life. You can maybe magic yourself a good grade
in your schoolwork, although it will still be vital to do the hard work and study as
well! You can also use it to get a Saturday job or find bargains when out shopping.

Abundance comes in many forms, but the important thing is that it must not
come at someone else's expense, and it must be able to make your life happier. It is
also good magical practice to give back a little of anything you have gained, so
perhaps find a charity to support.

Whatever the spell, magic works best when you provide it with a channel through which to work. Give it every opportunity to do its stuff. Maybe try entering some competitions, go into school with a bright and positive attitude, or start looking for a part-time job that may give you the first step on the ladder to your dream career.

The most important thing that runs through all these spells, however, is to think lucky—then you'll be lucky.

ABOVE Horseshoes are associated with luck.

TOP OF THE CLASS

A magical charm to help you overcome exam nerves

TO EARN GOOD GRADES, THERE IS NO SUBSTITUTE FOR BUCKLING DOWN TO HARD STUDY AND REVISION. EVEN THE MOST POWERFUL SPELL WILL NOT HELP YOU IF YOU SLACK OFF AT SCHOOL. HOWEVER, IF YOU HAVE DONE ALL THAT IS REQUIRED AND ARE STILL A BIT NERVOUS ABOUT HOW YOU'LL PERFORM ON YOUR EXAMS, USE THIS CHARM TO ATTAIN GOOD GRADES AND TAKE YOU TO THE TOP OF THE CLASS.

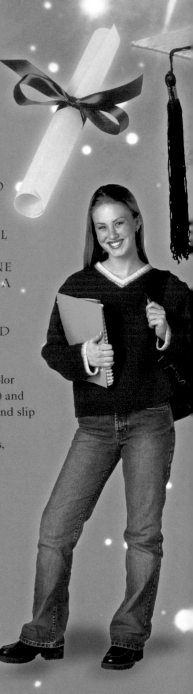

Light both of the candles (blue is the color associated with Jupiter, god of success) and the incense. Take up the piece of thread, and slip the buttons onto it, one by one, tying them securely in place as you do so. As you do this, recite the following chant:

With this first step, my place is secure
Worries about marks are no more

With the second step, true and strong,
In others' eyes I can do no wrong

With the third step, success is mine
Ever higher shall I climb

With this last step this spell is done
The highest grades shall be won!

Take the thread and buttons and place them in the bowl of earth, covering them as much as possible. Say:

This spell I bind by power of earth
That my success shall come to birth.

Retrieve the charm from the earth, brush it off as clean as you can, and place it in the matchbox. Put the matchbox in a special place along with the candles. Leave it undisturbed so that the magic can gather and work its power.

TAKE ...

A PIECE OF BLUE THREAD

4 ORANGE BUTTONS

2 BLUE CANDLES

INCENSE

A PINCH OF EARTH IN AN EARTHENWARE DISH

AN EMPTY MATCHBOX

MERLIN'S GOLD

*Let alchemy pave your path
with magical opportunities*

THIS SPELL IS BEST PERFORMED IN
THE SPRING SO THAT THE SEEDS CAN
BE PLANTED IN THE GARDEN. IF YOU
MUST PERFORM IT AT ANOTHER TIME,
OR IF THERE IS NO GARDEN AVAILABLE,
PLANT YOUR SEEDS IN A POT AND
KEEP THEM INDOORS INSTEAD.

TAKE ...

A PIECE OF PAPER

A SMALL PEBBLE

A GLASS OF WATER

*A GOLD-COLORED
    CANDLE*

*SOME
    FRANKINCENSE*

SOME SEEDS

A SUNNY DAY!

Take the piece of paper and draw upon it the
magical square of the sun, as shown right.
Place the pebble in the glass of water and stand it
on the paper in the sun. Let it absorb the sun's rays
for a few hours. In the evening, light a golden
candle and some incense. Take the pebble out of
the glass of water and place it on the paper

together with the seeds. If you are using a pot, have it handy. If you are planting the seeds in the garden, make sure that the ground is prepared.

Take a sip of the water and feel its golden energy surging through your body and transforming you. Say:

6	32	3	34	35	1
7	11	27	28	8	30
24	14	16	15	23	19
13	20	22	21	17	18
25	29	10	9	26	12
36	5	33	4	2	31

*By the power of the sun and by
    the might of the universe,
All that is plain shall turn
    to treasure;
All that is dull shall be
    bright.
By virtue of Merlin's magic,
My future shall be paved
With the gold of
    opportunities.
As I do will, so
    mote it be.*

Wrap the pebble in the paper and take the seeds in your hand. Place the wrapped stone in the earth and plant the seeds on top of it. As you do so, say:

*As a token of this spell,
I plant these seeds to show
How dross can turn to gold,
And so shall my life also grow
And be abundant
And blossom
From this moment on.
So mote it be.*

Finally, gently pour the rest of the water over the seeds.

MONEY SPINNER

Had bad luck? Here's how to rebuild your fortunes

EVERYONE HAS TIMES WHEN MONEY
IS IN SHORT SUPPLY, MAYBE THROUGH A
VENTURE THAT'S GONE WRONG OR BECAUSE
OF UNFORESEEN CIRCUMSTANCES. IF YOU
NEED TO RUSTLE UP SOME EXTRA CASH
AT A TIME OF HARDSHIP, THEN THIS
COULD BE THE SPELL FOR YOU.

Crush the mint leaves in your hand and add
them to the cup of boiling water. Drop the
coins in at this time also. For a few minutes, sit and
visualize exactly the amount of money you need.
Be realistic, however, because money spells tend
to give you what you need rather than what you
want. Visualize the money coming to you, say in
the form of extra pocket money or a gift. Then, start
to stir your tea in a clockwise direction saying:

Money, money, come to me—
Fortuna, bring me what I need.

Say it over and over again as you stir, keeping the visualization in your head at
all times. Then, when you start to feel a magical sense of calm certainty
steal over you, stop stirring and drink the tea, being careful not to swallow
the leaves or the coins. Once you have finished, take the coins and place
them in your pouch or change purse. You can also add
the mint leaves, once they have dried off. Keep
the pouch in a safe place. It may be prudent
for you to open up paths for the money to
come to you. For example, go for that
better-paying Saturday job, or offer to do

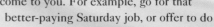

some chores for
your parents.
Magic works best
when it can operate
through opportunities
we create.

TAKE ...

A FEW LEAVES OF FRESH MINT

A CUP OF BOILING WATER

SOME SHINY COINS

A POUCH OR AN OLD CHANGE PURSE

SHOP TILL YOU DROP

A *special charm for successful shopping*

THERE ARE SOME PEOPLE WHO WILL NEVER BELIEVE IT, BUT SHOPPING IS SUCH HARD WORK! YOU GEAR YOURSELF UP TO GO OUT AND BUY SOMETHING IN PARTICULAR, AND WHEN YOU GET THERE THE ITEM IS EITHER GONE OR IS MORE EXPENSIVE THAN YOU FIRST THOUGHT. TO AVOID THESE PITFALLS, AND TO HELP YOU TO MAKE SENSIBLE SHOPPING DECISIONS, MAKE THIS CHARM AND CARRY IT WITH YOU WHENEVER YOU GO TO THE MALL.

The purse may be either bought or made, although self-made magical items always carry more personal power due to the work put into them. To make the purse even more special you could add some sequins in the shape of a pentagram to the outside. Your shopping symbols should reflect whatever it is you desire to buy. For example, if you are clothes shopping, then you could use some dolls' clothes, or if you want jewelry, use an old bracelet or ring. Alternatively, you could use pictures cut out from magazines.

Place the items and the piece of ginger (a plant to attract money and success) into the purse. Light the candle and spend a few minutes visualizing the things that you want to buy. See yourself

walking into the store and picking them up. When the
image is strong in your head, say:

Magic purse, by this deed
Bring me everything I need
Give the wisdom when I shop
Of when to buy and when to stop
Special bargains come my way
On my magic shopping day
Shake it once and shake it twice
The spell is alive
When I shake it thrice.

Shake the purse three times. The spell is now
activated and you may take the charm with you in your
handbag. Remember that you may have to change the items in the
purse and redo the spell every time you shop.

TAKE ...

A SMALL PURSE OF GOLDEN MATERIAL

SYMBOLS OF YOUR INTENDED SHOP

A SMALL PIECE OF ROOT
GINGER

A GREEN
CANDLE

THE PERFECT SATURDAY JOB

Get the job—and paycheck—you deserve

A LITTLE EXTRA MONEY WOULDN'T GO AMISS, SO
YOU DECIDE THAT A SATURDAY OR HOLIDAY JOB IS
JUST THE THING. THE TROUBLE IS, HOW DO YOU
GET THE ONE YOU WANT? THIS SPELL SHOULD HELP.

Perform this ritual on a Monday evening at the new moon. On an altar,
arrange the objects you need, placing the mirror in front of the candle
and the pin in front of the mirror. Light the candle and pass the pin through its
flame three times. Say:

O tool of the Art, I purify you in flame.
Be thou cleansed to do my bidding and hear my
*   charge this night.*

Then hold the pin gently in your hand,
over the mirror, and recite:

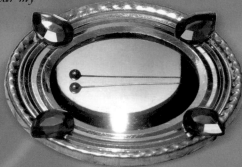

I charge thee by the powers that be
By the Ancient Gods and the spirits
*   that guide me*
Point the way to the job that is right
*   for me*
Put my feet upon the right path
And wherever thou art stuck
Lend your power and influence
So that I shall prevail
In my quest
And so art thou charged
In the names of the Old Ones
Blessed be thee.

TAKE ...

A NEW PIN

A SMALL MIRROR

A WHITE CANDLE

A PIECE OF SILK

Place the pin upon the mirror. This will help to magnify the spell and increase its power. Leave it there until the candle has burned down, then take the pin and wrap it carefully in the piece of silk. Then, when you see a job that you wish to apply for, take out the pin and stick it through a copy of the advertisement. If it was a verbal offer, write down a description of the position on a piece of paper. Put the paper and pin away safely but close to where you sleep.

LUCK, BE A LADY

A *winning charm for any game of chance*

THIS LITTLE BOX SPELL IS DESIGNED TO ATTRACT LUCK WHEN
ENTERING COMPETITIONS OR AT THE AMUSEMENT ARCADE.

Take the box and draw somewhere upon it the sign of Jupiter, the planet of
prosperity (see opposite, center). Place the rest of the ingredients into the box,
one by one, saying the appropriate chant as you do so:

For the coin:

Money, money, come to me
As I do will, so mote it be
Coins of silver, coins of gold
Make a fortune for my
  purse to hold.

For the cat's hair:

Hair of cat, black as night
Change my luck by this rite
Feline power shall bless
  this charm
So this spell shall cast
  no harm,

For the pair of dice:

Throw the dice, see them roll
And bring me luck to reach
  my goal
Of winning, winning all the way
This shall be my lucky day.

For the mint:

Little herb so pure so strong
Let my luck last true and long
My faith in magic never stint
And soon I know I'll make
  a mint.

Close the box and seal it either with tape or a piece of golden string. Give it a good shake and say:

Mixed together, my luck shall bring me money. In the name of the Old Ones, so mote it be.

Keep the luck-charged box near you when you enter those competitions. An alternative to the box is to make a blue or green pouch, embroidering the sign of Jupiter on the side. This pouch could then be easily carried to places requiring luck.

TAKE ...

A SMALL CARDBOARD BOX

A COIN

SOME HAIRS FROM A BLACK CAT (PREFERABLY SHED, NOT PLUCKED!)

A PAIR OF DICE

SOME DRIED MINT

A PEN

PIECE OF GOLDEN STRING

CAREER CHOOSER

Find the path to your ideal career

BEING SUCH A TALENTED INDIVIDUAL, IT IS SOMETIMES
HARD TO KNOW WHERE YOUR FUTURE LIES. IS IT IN
BANKING OR IN ACTING? OR MAYBE YOU SEE YOURSELF IN
THE HEADY WORLD OF PR? IF YOU ARE HAVING TROUBLE
DECIDING WHICH CAREER PATH TO FOLLOW, LET THE
SPIRITS HELP YOU TO DECIDE. TAKE YOUR TIME ON THIS
ONE THOUGH, AS SUCH DECISIONS ARE NOT A FRIVOLOUS
MATTER. YOU MAY EVEN FIND THAT YOUR HEART WILL
KNOW THE ANSWER WELL BEFORE THE SPELL IS COMPLETED.

Identify each stone with a certain career path. Spend a few days getting familiar
with the stones and thinking carefully about what each choice entails. See the
stone as embodying all the characteristics of the job. When you feel that you have
thought enough, take the stones out to your patch of earth. Make sure that it is a
calm day with no strong wind or breeze. Tie the string around the peg and place
the peg in the middle of the patch. Stretch the string out to the edge of the patch,
and, using the stick, draw a circle in the dirt. Next, divide the circle into as many
sections as you have stones and place one stone in each division.

Take the crow's feather. Crows have always been associated with prophecy and
seeing into the unknown. Hold the feather above the center point and say:

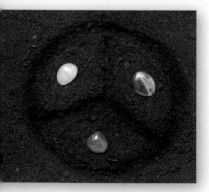

*Spirits that help me, that walk by my side, I ask
now for your help. Guardian spirits, guide this
feather so that it may help me choose a special path
for my future. I will consider your choice with an
open heart and an open mind, honoring the wisdom
that you bring from your world.*

Let go of the feather and let it drift earthward. Where
it lands is where the spirits have indicated your future
path may lie. Gather up the stones, scuff out the circle,
and remember to thank the spirits for their help.

TAKE ...

A DIFFERENT STONE FOR EACH TYPE OF CAREER YOU
   ARE INTERESTED IN

A CROW'S FEATHER (SMOOTH AND UNBROKEN)

A PATCH OF EARTH, NO LESS THAN 3 FT (1M) SQUARE

A PEG

A PIECE OF STRING

A STICK

TRIED AND TESTED

SPORTS TEAMS HAVE MASCOTS FOR GOOD LUCK. YOU
CAN HAVE ONE, TOO. MASCOTS MAKE US FEEL ASSURED
WHEN LIFE SEEMS UNCERTAIN, OR WHEN WE'RE FACING
AN UNUSUAL, CHALLENGING, OR STRESSFUL SITUATION.
NOW YOU CAN MAKE YOUR OWN FRIENDLY MASCOT,
AND IMBUE IT WITH MAGIC POWER.

Draw a circle on the paper with the pen. Make it large enough for your mascot
to fit inside. Next, take your mascot and place it in the center of the
circle. Light the candle and incense and place them at the back of the
circle so that you will not catch yourself on them by accident. Place
the dishes of water and earth to the front, so that all the elements
form a square around the circle.

Pick up the mascot and wave it over the candle flame
(carefully so that you don't set it or yourself on fire!). Say:

*By the power of fire, I charge you with my will. Bring
to me calmness and confidence when I need it most.*

Next, pass the mascot through the incense smoke and say:

*By the power of air, I breathe life into you. Send to me
calmness and confidence when I need it most.*

Sprinkle the mascot with water, saying:

*By the power of water, the energy of the universe flows through you,
bringing me calmness and confidence when I need it most.*

Place the mascot on the dish of earth. Say:

*Power of earth, steady my will. Bring to birth this charm so that I
may always have calmness and confidence when I need it most.*

TAKE ...

*A SMALL MASCOT (SUCH AS A
   SMALL CUDDLY TOY, A SMOOTH
   PEBBLE, OR A CRYSTAL)*

A CANDLE

*A SMALL BOWL
   OF WATER*

INCENSE

SOME EARTH

*A PIECE OF
   PAPER AND A
   PEN*

Replace the mascot in the center of the circle and place your hands upon it. For a few
moments visualize yourself walking into situations where you will require calmness
and confidence, such as interviews or exams. See yourself carrying your mascot and
radiating a sense of quiet self-assurance. When the picture is clear in your mind, bring
the mascot up to your lips and breathe softly on it. Say:

*I name you — [choose a name].You are now my friend and my aid until I say
   otherwise. So mote it be.*

LOVE
AND
SCENTUALITY

HOW TO BE A REAL BABE

EVERYONE WANTS TO BE LOVED. LOVE COMES IN MANY
FORMS AND IN DIFFERENT INTENSITIES, BUT, WHEN MOST
PEOPLE THINK OF LOVE, THEY THINK OF THAT BETWEEN A
COUPLE. LOVE SPELLS HAVE ALWAYS BEEN ONE OF THE MOST
POPULAR TYPES OF ENCHANTMENT AND HAVE CAUGHT THE
HUMAN IMAGINATION LIKE NO OTHER. MAGICAL POWERS
CAN CERTAINLY DRAW TWO SOULS TOGETHER, BUT THE PATH
OF TRUE LOVE IS NOT, ALAS, ALWAYS SMOOTH.

Again, there are rules for this kind of spellcasting for it would be very easy to
work unethically when it comes to matters of the heart. First, you should never
try to influence someone to love you against their will—the chances are this won't
work anyway. Instead, use magic to improve the way
they see you. Then, in the future, who can tell what
will happen between you? Spells should not cause
harm to others. Therefore, never set out to enchant
someone who is already in a relationship, no matter
how convinced you are that they are unhappy where
they are. Such magic can end up binding you in more
misery than you can ever know.

On the positive side, if you wish to draw a
soul mate to you, or to repair a love that has

All my
love

xxxo

gone wrong, you can use magic to ease the way. I find that such spells work in their own time and way so that sometimes you will meet the person of your dreams where and when you least expect it to happen. Then, when you find your true love, wow them with your magical kisses and keep them true to you with the Fidelity Knot. Then, even if after all your attempts, fate decrees against the relationship, use spellcraft to heal your broken heart.

KISS ME QUICK!

Become the best kisser in town

NO MORE PRACTICING ON THE
BACK OF YOUR HAND OR THE
MIRROR. THIS SUREFIRE SPELL WILL
MAKE YOU THE BEST KISSER FOR MILES
AROUND. USING THE SIMPLEST OF INGREDIENTS, YOU WILL
SOON HAVE THE CONFIDENCE TO PUCKER UP TO YOUR
LOVED ONE KNOWING THAT YOUR LUSCIOUS LIPS ARE JUST
ONE STEP AWAY FROM A HEAVENLY EXPERIENCE. BUT
BEWARE, ALTHOUGH THIS MAY MAKE YOU A GREAT KISSER,
IT MAY NOT IMPROVE THE SKILLS OF YOUR PARTNER!

On the night of a bright full moon, leave your lipstick in a place where it can
absorb the powerful lunar energy. Next, either with the pen, or, if you prefer,
with a penknife, mark the lipstick with three Xs, like this:

XXX

This symbol, apart from being used to
represent a kiss, is also the rune for
a blessing or a gift. And gifted is
most certainly what you should be
after this spell! Hold the lipstick
close to your heart and repeat the
following words:

*By earth and air, by fire
and water. By sun and
moon and stars. By standing
trees and bursting buds. By*

flowers and leaves and fruit. By all that flies, swims, walks, and crawls, I charge this lipstick that it should become a tool of love. Whenever I wear it, may I become confident that my kisses will be as sweet as the summer rain and as hot as fire. And may no harm befall any through this spell.

Apply the lipstick as you would if you were going out and press your lips against the paper, leaving a picture of your "kiss." Underneath it, write the words you spoke just now to remind you of the magic you have just performed, and then stow the paper away in a place where no one else will find it. This spell should be renewed every three months until you feel your confidence has grown to such an extent that you no longer need it.

TAKE ...

AN UNUSED LIPSTICK

A PIECE OF BLANK PAPER

A PEN

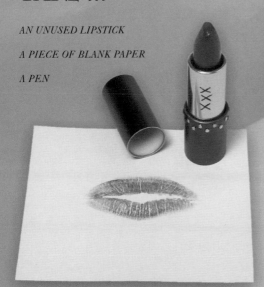

LOVE STARTER

*A charm for enchanting
the new love in your life*

AT THE START OF A
RELATIONSHIP YOU WILL WANT YOUR
NEW BOYFRIEND TO WORSHIP THE GROUND YOU WALK ON.
THE LOVE STARTER CAN ALSO BE USED TO HELP RENEW AN
OLD RELATIONSHIP, BUT ONLY IF BOTH PARTNERS COME
TOGETHER IN HONESTY AND WITHOUT REGRETS.

Enchant your beloved with this simple spell, which is best performed at, or as close as possible to, the new moon. An apple is used here, because apples are one of the fruits beloved of Aphrodite, the Greek goddess of love. In many old stories and legends the fruit has become associated with romance and passion.

When you are next with your new love, take a rosy red apple, core it (but save the core!), and then slice it in half. Give half to the new person in your life and then eat the other half yourself. Later, try to be alone so that you can bury the core in your garden. Once it is safely back in the womb of the earth, surround the site with the stones, to mark it as a place of enchantment.

Sit back and croon quietly

to yourself the words below.
See them as a powerful energy
force coming from your mouth
and infusing the area of earth
around the apple core with
magic. Keep singing until you
feel the magic has taken effect.

Love will grow,
Sure and slow,
Strong and true,
This love will prove.

Then, every evening for the next seven days,
return to the spot. Touch each of the seven
stones in turn and say:

May our love have the strength of a tree,
Be as flexible as boughs in the wind,
Be as sweet as its fruit.
May our blessing be as many as the leaves,
And may it be nurtured by the powers of both
heaven and earth.
If it harm none,
So mote it be.

TAKE ...

1 RED APPLE

7 SMALL PINK OR RED
STONES

LOVE FIZZLER

A bewitching bath fizzler to make you truly irresistible

THIS EASY-TO-MAKE BATHTIME CHARM WILL GIVE YOUR LOVE LIFE A BOOST BY TURNING YOU INTO THE MOST IRRESISTIBLE PERSON ON THE PLANET! TO THE BASIC RECIPE FOR A BATH FIZZLER ARE ADDED THE MAGICAL ENERGIES OF JASMINE OIL AND CINNAMON FOR LOVE AND ATTRACTION, AND OF COURSE, YOUR OWN WILLPOWER.

Place the first four dry ingredients into the bowl and stir until they are well blended. In a separate dish, pour the essential oil of jasmine and the food coloring into the almond oil until the oil is evenly infused with both the color and the scent. Then slowly add the oil mixture to the dry ingredients, making sure to stir it clockwise. As you stir, say:

Stir the potion around and around.
In this circle of Venus love shall abound.
Make me a goddess of desire
To set all suitors' hearts afire.
May this spell imprisoned be
Till power of water sets it free.

Keep adding the oil and stirring until the mixture is the consistency of pastry dough. Then take small scoops, about 1 inch (2.5 centimeters) in diameter and shape them either into balls, or, if you are creative, into little hearts. Place them on a piece of waxed paper to dry out and harden. This should take between one to two days. When they are dry, wrap them ready for use in small pieces of waxed paper and store them in an airtight jar. Use between one and three at a time just before that big date.

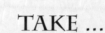

TAKE ...

2 TABLESPOONS CITRIC ACID

2 TABLESPOONS CORNSTARCH

¼ CUP BAKING SODA

A PINCH OF CINNAMON

4–5 DROPS OF ESSENTIAL OIL OF JASMINE

3–6 DROPS OF RED FOOD COLORING

3 TABLESPOONS PURE ALMOND OIL

A MIXING BOWL AND A SMALL DISH

A SPOON

SOME WAXED PAPER

RELATIONSHIP BOOSTER

Banish problems from your relationship and restore harmony

EVEN THE BEST RELATIONSHIPS HAVE MOMENTS WHEN THINGS DON'T RUN AS SMOOTHLY AS THEY SHOULD. IF THIS IS THE CASE FOR YOU, TRY THIS SIMPLE PIECE OF MAGIC WITH EARTH AND WATER.

First, find yourself a small, smooth, black pebble, one that you like the feel of. Stones are allied to earth magic—the magic of stability and prosperity. Stones also have the ability to absorb energies, especially thoughts and feelings. The color black increases the stone's receptive powers. Before you use the pebble, silently ask its permission and for its help in solving your problems. You will know intuitively if the stone agrees to be your ally.

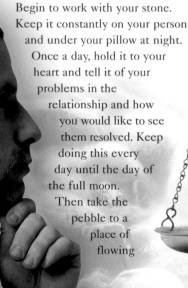

Begin to work with your stone. Keep it constantly on your person and under your pillow at night. Once a day, hold it to your heart and tell it of your problems in the relationship and how you would like to see them resolved. Keep doing this every day until the day of the full moon. Then take the pebble to a place of flowing

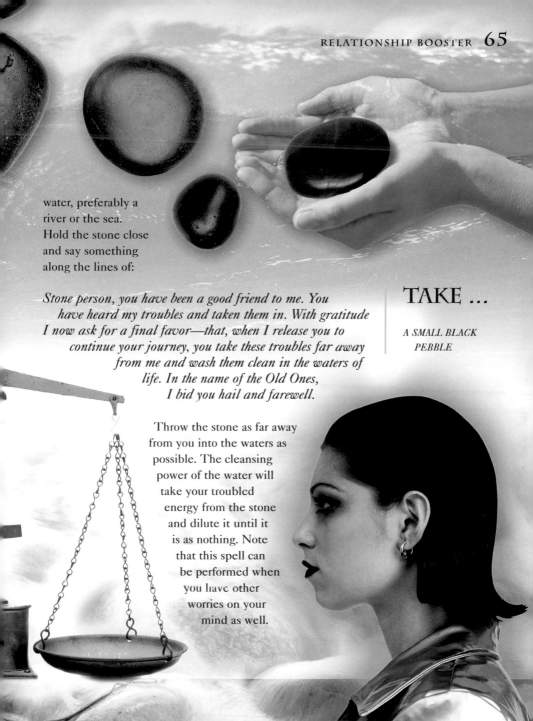

water, preferably a river or the sea. Hold the stone close and say something along the lines of:

Stone person, you have been a good friend to me. You have heard my troubles and taken them in. With gratitude I now ask for a final favor—that, when I release you to continue your journey, you take these troubles far away from me and wash them clean in the waters of life. In the name of the Old Ones, I bid you hail and farewell.

TAKE ...

A SMALL BLACK PEBBLE

Throw the stone as far away from you into the waters as possible. The cleansing power of the water will take your troubled energy from the stone and dilute it until it is as nothing. Note that this spell can be performed when you have other worries on your mind as well.

I WANT YOU BACK

*If true love has to be rekindled,
this is the spell to do it*

RELATIONSHIPS, LIKE ANY OTHER LIVING, GROWING
THING, HAVE THEIR NATURAL TIME SPANS. SOME LAST
A LIFETIME, OTHERS ONLY DAYS, WEEKS, OR MONTHS.
IT IS IMPORTANT TO KNOW WHEN TO LET GO AND
START ANEW. HOWEVER, OCCASIONALLY YOU MAY FEEL
THAT A RELATIONSHIP IS WORTH A SECOND TRY.

Think carefully about this first. Ponder the reasons for the break and whether
you really want to go there again. More importantly, how will your magic
affect the other person? It is not ethical to use magic to influence someone against
their will. So before you use this spell take all these things into consideration.

If you decide to go ahead, choose a Friday evening as close as possible to the
new moon. Prepare yourself with a bath and clean clothes or robes. The candles need
to be placed somewhere where they do not need to be moved or cleared away. If you
can do this on your altar, fine; if not, find another safe place such as a mantelpiece or

cold fire grate. Position them about 9 inches (23 centimeters) apart and stand your photo behind one and the other person's photo behind the other. Attach the silver thread to both candles by tying it near the base. Light the candles, then say three times:

This candle for him,
This candle for me.
When they touch,
Reunited we'll be.
Rekindle the love,
Rekindle the flame—
— [insert your lover's name], I call your name.

Move the candle representing the other person 1 inch (2.5 centimeters) closer to yours. Do this by carefully rotating it so that the thread winds around its base. Repeat this procedure for the next eight days, by which time the candles should touch. Wrap the remains of the candles, the thread, and the photos in a soft pink cloth and store in a safe place.

TAKE ...

2 WHITE CANDLES

A SILVER THREAD

A PHOTO OF THE OBJECT OF YOUR
LOVE

A PHOTO OF YOU

TO HEAL A BROKEN HEART

A *spell to help you move on when a relationship is over*

THE COURSE OF TRUE LOVE NEVER DOES
RUN SMOOTHLY. HOW EASY IT IS TO FALL
HEAD OVER HEELS ONLY TO BE DUMPED
WHEN YOU LEAST EXPECT IT. IF THIS HAS
HAPPENED TO YOU AND YOU FEEL AS IF
YOUR HEART IS BROKEN, USE THIS SPELL
TO START THE HEALING PROCESS. WITHIN
A SHORT PERIOD OF TIME, YOU'LL BE BACK
TO YOUR OLD SELF AGAIN.

Preferably at the time of the new moon, find a quiet place where you can light a candle and the incense. Take the stick and break it in half. Say:

This broken stick represents my broken heart and my sadness. What was once whole and healthy is now hurt and bewildered. I bring my heart to this place at this time so that it may start its journey toward healing and finding true love once more.

Start to wrap the wool around the two parts of stick, fastening them tightly together, saying:

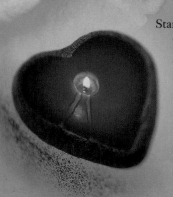

*With this wool, I bind what is broken
A soothing balm of words to be spoken
I am the healer of my own heart
From this moment my healing shall start.*

Once the sticks are bound together it is time to entreat the powers of the four elements to help you in your magic. First, carefully hold the sticks over the candle (make sure that they will not catch on fire) and say:

Powers of fire, bring warmth back to my heart again.

Next, hold the stick in the smoke of the incense and say:

Powers of air, breathe a new hope of future love my way.

Then sprinkle some earth over the stick, saying:

Powers of earth, give stability back to my life again.

Now take your stick to a place of flowing water, such as a stream, river, or the sea, and throw it in as far as it will go. As you do so, say these final words:

Powers of water take this symbol of my broken heart and cleanse it of all hurting words and deeds. May I feel the touch of your healing magic within me as the moon turns her cycle in the sky. By the powers of the Old Ones, so mote it be.

TAKE …

A THIN STICK OR TWIG

SOME BLUE WOOL

INCENSE

A BLUE CANDLE

A BOWL OF EARTH

FIDELITY KNOT

Tie the knot to keep the bonds of fidelity firm

NOW THAT YOU HAVE GOT YOUR BOYFRIEND, YOU WANT
TO HANG ON. THIS SPELL WILL ENCOURAGE FIDELITY.
BUT BEWARE OF THAT LITTLE GREEN-EYED MONSTER OF
JEALOUSY—IT CAN HAVE YOU IMAGINING ALL SORTS OF
THINGS THAT MAY NOT REALLY BE HAPPENING, AND THAT
IN ITSELF COULD PUSH YOUR LOVE AWAY.

O n the night of the full moon set up your
altar and light the two green candles and
the incense. Start to fashion a human shape of
the pipe cleaner, making it as realistic as
you can. When you have done your best
to form it into a recognizably human
shape, cut out the face of your
beloved from the photo and
attach it to the pipe cleaner
figure's head. As you do so,
clearly visualize the pipe
cleaner figure
becoming real,
taking on the
features and habits
of your beloved.
When the picture
has strongly formed in your
head, take the green
ribbon and tie it around
the figure's hips,
fastening it in a tight
double bow. As you do
so, say these words:

TAKE ...

A PIPE CLEANER

A SMALL PHOTO OF YOUR BELOVED

A PIECE OF GREEN RIBBON

2 GREEN CANDLES

YOUR FAVORITE INCENSE

Figurine, for this spell, you are he.
I name you — [insert your beloved's name].
This spell shall command him,
As it commands you.
With this ribbon your heart is tied to mine;
With this ribbon your body is
tied to mine.
I say to you, do not stray—
Faithful to my love you
shall stay
Till the mountains
crumble,
Till the stars burn out,
Or until I undo you.
This is my will—
So mote it be.

Keep the figure in a
safe place. However,
bear in mind that other,
stronger magic may be at
work that will render this
charm useless. If it is fate
that he is not to be with you,
accept it and let him go.

BEAUTY

AND

BODY

PAMPER YOUR HEAVENLY BODY

ABOVE Traditionally witches were pictured as ugly old women. Of course, we know that isn't true today.

THE TRADITIONAL IMAGE OF A WITCH LEAVES A LOT TO BE DESIRED WHEN IT COMES TO THE BEAUTY STAKES. AFTER ALL, WHO NEEDS BLACK TEETH AND A WARTY CHIN WHEN THEY CAN TURN THEMSELVES INTO A FEMME FATALE. THE HISTORY MAKERS OF YESTERYEAR ALWAYS TOOK PAINS TO SHOW WITCHES AS UGLY OLD WOMEN EVEN WHEN MANY OF THOSE TRIED FOR WITCHCRAFT WERE YOUNG.

The idea was that, because magic was considered by the Christian Church to be a bad thing, then those who practiced it would become twisted by their own evil. In these more enlightened times few people who know anything about witchcraft believe it to be nasty or wicked. Many practitioners are young and, whatever their shape, size, color, or (if they have one) creed, they have a beauty about them that comes from an inner knowledge of their own uniqueness in the universe.

This chapter combines ways of finding this inner beauty with recipes for potions and lotions to enhance your outer beauty. Herbal recipes have been used since ancient times to make the hair shine and the skin glow.

Pampering yourself in these ways will make you feel more special, which in turn will help to affirm that you are a beautiful person in your own eyes. Once you truly believe in your own beauty it will shine out from you, and others will believe in it, too. You do not have to start out looking like a Barbie doll; you do not have to go on a crash diet; nor do you have to undergo cosmetic surgery. Just use some of the spells here, or maybe develop your own. Trust me— once you believe you are beautiful, at that instant you shall be.

ABOVE Many beauty potions use easily available ingredients from around the home.

ABOVE Mixing your own potions will make you feel special.

MY BODY, MY TEMPLE

Empower your mind and increase your body strength with healing goddess energy

THE SEVEN CHAKRAS ARE ENERGY SYSTEMS WITHIN THE HUMAN AURIC FIELD, AND THEIR PURPOSE IS TO ABSORB, TRANSFORM, AND DISTRIBUTE THE UNIVERSAL ENERGY. THE TERM CHAKRA MEANS "WHEEL," AND ESOTERIC TRADITION IN BOTH THE EAST AND WEST USES THE CONCEPT OF CHAKRAS FOR ENERGIZING THE PERSON. THIS VISUALIZATION EXERCISE WILL GIVE YOU A SPIRITUAL ENERGY BOOST.

Sit comfortably on the cushion and make sure that you cannot be disturbed. For a few minutes concentrate on relaxing your whole body and making your breathing slow and deep. As you inhale, imagine your body pulling up energy from the depths of Mother Earth. This energy, golden in color, rises through your body and travels from the base of your spine upward. As it does this it is going to energize the seven main chakras, or energy centers of your body. For the purpose of this exercise it will be easiest to imagine your chakras as different-colored flowers.

Breathing in, the energy rises to your first chakra. This is the base chakra, situated at the base of your spine. Red in color, it represents the basic life force of your body. See the energy touching the chakra's closed flower bud and, as it does so, watch it unfurl into a beautiful red flower.

Breathing in again, pull the power up further to just below your navel. This is the site of the second chakra, the center of sexual energy and creativity. It is orange in color. Once again, watch it unfurl into a glorious bloom. Repeat the breathing in and watching the flower open for each of the chakras listed opposite.

Once you reach the Crown Chakra, imagine the energy bursting forth and falling back to the earth again, rather like a fountain. Once you have done this for a while, close the chakra centers by imagining a gentle silver rain falling on and

✳ **5TH CHAKRA**
base of throat
blue
communication

✳ **4TH CHAKRA**
heart
green
love and friendship

✳ **6TH CHAKRA**
middle of forehead/
third eye
indigo
*mental abilities/intuition/
psychic powers*

✳ **3RD CHAKRA**
solar plexus
yellow
*relationship with
the world*

✳ **7TH CHAKRA**
immediately above
the top of the head
multicolored lotus
spirituality

✳ **2ND CHAKRA**
below the navel
orange
*center of sexual energy
and creativity*

✳ **1ST CHAKRA**
base of spine
red
your body's life force

cleansing each one, closing it again into a bud.
Always close the chakras before going out into the
world, as "open" chakras can sometimes pick up
undesirable energies.

TAKE ...

A COMFORTABLE CUSHION

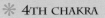

FACE MAGIC

An ancient spell to enhance the beauty of your face, eyes, and lips.

THIS IS JUST THE THING FOR THE NIGHT OF THE BIG PARTY—
A SPELL TO ENHANCE YOUR NATURAL BEAUTY AND LEAVE YOU
WITH IMMEDIATE RADIANCE AND WONDERFULLY SOFT SKIN.
THIS IS AN OLD BEAUTY SPELL FOR THE SKIN, EYES, AND LIPS;
IT WAS GIVEN TO ME BY A WOMAN WHOSE FAMILY HAVE
BEEN GREEN WITCHES SINCE TIME IMMEMORIAL.

First, a note on the main ingredients. Strawberry leaves
have long been used in skin recipes, as have marigold
petals and elderflowers. They all have toning and healing
properties that bring the skin alive. The rosewater, too,
is a skin tonic used in many ancient beauty remedies.
As for the brandy, it is used here as a preservative, so
that your magical mixture will last.

On the night of a clear
full moon, gather the
ingredients listed. Place
each of the herbs in one
of three different bowls.
Crush the leaves and petals
slightly to bruise them
before pouring over about
a cupful of boiling water.
Leave the herbs to infuse
for nine minutes, then
strain the remaining
infusions into one large
bowl or jar. Leave to cool
before adding the rosewater
and brandy. Finally, add the
magical ingredient of

TAKE ...

*2 TABLESPOONS OF STRAWBERRY
LEAVES*

*2 TABLESPOONS OF MARIGOLD
PETALS*

*2 TABLESPOONS OF
ELDERFLOWERS*

ROSEWATER

*8 TEASPOONS BRANDY (ASK
YOUR PARENTS!)*

*A THIMBLEFUL OF
MORNING DEW
(COLLECT IT EARLY
AND SAVE IT UNTIL
THE EVENING)*

morning dew, said by
ancient legend to bestow
the gift of beauty on
whoever bathes in it.
Take the jar outside into the
moonlight. At some secluded spot,
where the light of the moon can
shine on it, put the pot down,
then kneel beside it. Say:

*Fair moon goddess and
Faery folk,
Bestow on me a boon
this night,
That this potion be
enchanted
By elven dust and
silver light.
For softened skin
so beautiful,
Charmed be these
three herbs true-
A face so fair to behold
By rosewater and
morning dew.*

Go to bed, but make sure you rise
before dawn so that no sunlight falls
upon your magical potion. Decant it into
a dark glass bottle and keep in a dark
cupboard to preserve its magical
powers. To use, dampen a clean
wad of cotton or cotton ball
with the mixture and
apply to your face every
day and before a
special event.

SPOT BE GONE

Banish those spots before a big day

YOU KNOW HOW IT IS.
IN THE DAYS LEADING UP
TO A BIG DATE OR A DANCE YOU
SUDDENLY FEEL THE DREADED ITCHING
OF A NEW BLEMISH OR PIMPLE COMING
THROUGH, RIGHT WHERE IT WILL BE
MOST OBVIOUS. AND YOU ALSO KNOW
THAT ITS TIMING IS IMPECCABLE: IT WILL BE AT ITS
REDDEST AND LUMPIEST ON YOUR BIG DAY. DON'T
DESPAIR; TRY THIS OLD COUNTRY REMEDY AS
SOON AS YOU SEE THE FIRST SIGNS.

Take the potato, wash it well, and then cut it in half. Take one of the halves and press it against the affected spot (the potato juice is also good for the skin). Say:

Spot, spot, get thee out.

Repeat this three times while "feeling" the spot being drawn out of your skin and into the potato. Don't rush this part—give it time to work. Then take your potato and dig a deep hole in the ground. Place the potato in it and sprinkle it with the cleansing power of the salt. As you fill in the hole, chant:

Unwelcome spot get thee away
Blemish shall not spoil the day
Thou art buried in this spot
And in darkness you shall rot.

The theory behind this spell is that
as the potato decays back into
Mother Earth, so too shall the "spot"
wither and disappear from your face.

TAKE ...

A SMALL POTATO

SOME SALT

CROWNING GLORY

An old Gypsy charm for lustrous shine and to speed up hair growth

THIS SPECIAL OLD RECIPE FOR SHAMPOO
CONTAINS INGREDIENTS THAT WILL LEAVE
YOUR HAIR LUSTROUS AND STRONG. AN
ADDED BENEFIT IS THAT IT IS ALSO ANTI-
DANDRUFF AND PROMOTES HAIR GROWTH.
AND, AS USUAL, THERE IS AN ADDED MAGICAL
INGREDIENT JUST TO MAKE IT A LITTLE OUT
OF THE ORDINARY!

Bring the water to boil in a large saucepan, adding the
herbs. Take off the burner, stir, and leave to infuse in
the water for three hours. Then take the mixture and strain
the liquid into another saucepan. Put the used herbs to one
side. Into the saucepan of herbal liquid, add the shredded
soap and place over a low heat. Stir vigorously until the soap
dissolves. Take off the burner once again, and add the borax.
Next, as it is cooling, sprinkle over the maidenhair dust.
Maidenhair's magical properties are supposed to convey
beauty onto whoever wears it. Stir the powder
clockwise, chanting:

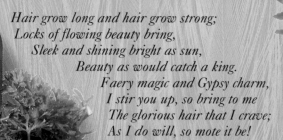

Hair grow long and hair grow strong;
Locks of flowing beauty bring,
Sleek and shining bright as sun,
Beauty as would catch a king.
Faery magic and Gypsy charm,
I stir you up, so bring to me
The glorious hair that I crave;
As I do will, so mote it be!

Let the mixture cool before bottling
and labeling it. Leave it to stand

for 24 hours. Meanwhile, take the used herbs and dispose of them accordingly. This does not mean throwing them in the trash. Instead, take them into the garden, dig a small hole, and give them back to Mother Earth. Leave a small offering of thanks such as a piece of your hair.

When you come to use the mixture, remember to give it a good shake first to remix the ingredients, which will have settled in the meantime. Add a small amount to your wet hair and massage it in well. Leave it on for five more minutes before rinsing in cool water.

TAKE ...

A HANDFUL OF THE FRESH TOPS OF YOUNG NETTLES

A HANDFUL OF FRESH PARSLEY

A HANDFUL OF FRESH ROSEMARY

3 PINTS OF BOILING WATER

6 TABLESPOONS OF SHREDDED CASTILE SOAP

1 TABLESPOON OF BORAX

A PINCH OF DRIED MAIDENHAIR FERN, GROUND TO A POWDER

CLEOPATRA'S OIL

A powerful Egyptian beauty potion favored by this most infamous enchantress

THE WOMEN OF ANCIENT EGYPT WERE AS ANXIOUS TO STAY BEAUTIFUL AS ARE WOMEN OF TODAY. OLD DRAWINGS AND TEXTS FROM TOMBS GIVE US AN IDEA OF WHAT INGREDIENTS THEY USED FOR THEIR TOILETRIES AND MAKEUP. THEY LIKED TO KEEP CLEAN AND OFTEN USED HEAVILY SCENTED OILS TO PERFUME THEIR HAIR AND BODIES. HERE'S A MOISTURIZING AND NOURISHING PREPARATION FOR THE BODY BEAUTIFUL.

Perhaps the most famous Egyptian woman of all was Queen Cleopatra, that legendary temptress of the Nile. She is supposed to have bathed in asses' milk to remain beautiful, although the recipe on the right is supposed to have been her favorite soak. Whether or not it is true, the ingredients above are rich, exotic, and full of goodness for the skin. It will certainly make you feel like a queen. As this mixture costs more to prepare than normal bath oils, save it for special occasions— perhaps before that essential spell you have to cast.

Crack the egg into a bowl and add the olive, palm, and almond oils and the honey. Whisk these together until well mixed and then add the essential oils, alcohol, milk, and soap flakes. Remember, though: It is essential to keep whisking while adding these ingredients. Once all the ingredients are well mixed, pour them into a bottle, label it, then keep it in the refrigerator. It should be used up within a week.

When you come to pour it into the tub, make sure that the water is not too hot and that you add it to the water slowly. Then switch off the telephone, light a candle, step into the silky-soft water, and time-warp yourself back to ancient Egypt!

TAKE ...

1 EGG

8 TABLESPOONS MILK

8 TABLESPOONS OLIVE OIL

4 TABLESPOONS ALMOND OIL

4 TABLESPOONS PALM OIL

1 TEASPOON HONEY

4 TABLESPOONS ALCOHOL

1 TEASPOON MILD SOAP FLAKES

1 DROP EACH OF ESSENTIAL OILS OF CEDARWOOD, FRANKINCENSE, AND SANDALWOOD

MIRROR, MIRROR

A beauty spell worth reflecting on!

WE ALL KNOW THE STORY OF SNOW
WHITE. HER WICKED STEPMOTHER
KEPT A MAGIC MIRROR TO MAKE SURE
THAT SHE WAS THE FAIREST IN THE LAND. YOU,
TOO, CAN USE A MIRROR TO ENHANCE YOUR
BEAUTY ALTHOUGH IT WILL NOT TALK TO YOU AS
IN THE FAIRY TALE AND IT WILL NOT CAUSE YOU TO
GO OUT AND SLAY ANYONE YOU THINK IS MORE BEAUTIFUL!

This spell is designed to let you see your true beauty, from the inside out. Once you have learned to radiate this inner beauty, or, as some witches describe it, put on a "glamour," it will not matter if you normally think yourself as ugly or overweight, too short or too tall; you will attract all around you like moths to a candle.

Make the infusion by pouring boiling water on the clary sage leaves and leave until cooled. Clary sage is an herb that is said to improve sight, and that includes third-eye sight, too! Strain the liquid into a bowl and wipe over the surface of the mirror while chanting:

Mirror, mirror, clear
your sight;
Show my true self by this rite;
From the castle of my soul
An inner beauty to behold.

Put on your favorite clothes and makeup, and style your hair the way you like it. Then stand in front of the mirror and stare into your own eyes. Keep this up until you feel you are being absorbed into the mirror. At this point, visualize yourself reaching deep inside and bringing out your inner beauty. Now look at yourself again and this time really admire the way you look: see how your skin radiates, how your eyes beckon. Say to yourself:

I am beautiful, I am unique. However I am made,
I know that my beauty reaches out from within. So mote it be.

This spell is great done just before you go out, because it boosts self-confidence. It is also a cumulative spell—the more you do it, the better it gets!

TAKE ...

A MIRROR

AN INFUSION OF
CLARY SAGE

BRIGHT EYES

Bring the sparkle back to tired eyes

THIS SPELL FOR CLEAR, REFRESHED EYES
USES A COMBINATION OF AN HERBAL
BEAUTY RECIPE AND A MAGIC CHARM TO
GIVE IT MORE POTENCY. THE RAINWATER,
STRAIGHT FROM THE SKY, BRINGS MAGICAL
QUALITIES OF ITS OWN, MIXED BETWEEN HEAVEN AND
EARTH. IF YOU ARE UNABLE TO OBTAIN ALL THE HERBAL
INGREDIENTS OPPOSITE, DON'T WORRY: THE SPELL WILL
WORK JUST AS WELL WITH TWO OR THREE OF THEM.

Place the dried flowers into a bowl and mix them thoroughly with your hand.
Tip the rainwater into a stainless steel saucepan (any other metal may taint
the water) and slowly bring to a boil. When it has reached this point, carefully pour the
water over the flowers and leave the mixture until it has cooled completely. Strain
the dried matter from the liquid and pour the liquid back into the bowl. Carefully
place the citrine crystal into the potion you have made. Say:

Eyes be clear and eyes be bright
May magic charm my powers of sight
Beautiful eyes that shine like the sun
With crystal power my will be done.

Leave the crystal in the eye potion for a day and a night, then take it out and pour
the liquid into a glass bottle. To use, dampen two cotton balls and place them over
your closed eyes. Lie down and relax like this for about 10 minutes morning and
evening, or before you are due to go
out. This mixture should be used
up within a week.

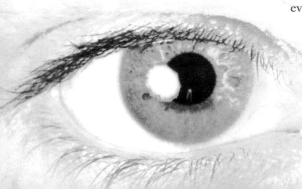

TAKE ...

*RAINWATER, COLLECTED
  IN A CUP*

*A TABLESPOON OF DRIED
  CHAMOMILE FLOWERS*

*A TABLESPOON OF DRIED
  CORNFLOWERS*

*A TABLESPOON OF DRIED
  ELDERFLOWERS*

*A TEASPOON OF DRIED
  EYEBRIGHT*

A CITRINE CRYSTAL

SOME COTTON BALLS

SPIRIT
POWER

TRAIN YOUR PSYCHIC POWERS

WE ALL HAVE THE POTENTIAL OF PSYCHIC POWER WITHIN US, WHETHER WE ARE CONSCIOUS OF IT OR NOT. HOW MANY TIMES HAVE YOU HAD AN INSTINCT THAT SOMETHING WAS GOING TO HAPPEN JUST BEFORE IT DID? SOME PEOPLE HAVE GUIDING DREAMS THAT GIVE THEM CLUES AS TO WHAT FUTURE PATH TO FOLLOW. OTHERS MAY BE SURPRISED BY THE NUMBER OF "COINCIDENCES" THAT KEEP CROPPING UP IN THEIR LIVES.

Humans are certainly more than the sum of their physical parts and anyone who wishes to become a spellcaster will soon need to get acquainted with their psychic side. A good way to begin is to develop the subconscious through visualization work and guided meditations (such as the Meet Your Spirit Guide meditation).

Visualization strengthens the inner eye and is a more intense form of daydreaming—incorporating every sense. This skill is vital to spellcasting, because it focuses the will on your goal. And, of course, the basis of all magic is strength of will over matter.

Guided meditations are forms of visualizations where you take a "journey" in your mind's eye. This journey can be one of your own imagining or it can be one that you listen to and follow on a prerecorded cassette or CD. Such visualizations open up your inner worlds, where you will encounter symbolic scenes or will meet spirit guides essential to your spiritual development. Meeting the inhabitants of other worlds may not be easy at first, but persevere—the effort will be well worth it.

On the other hand, you may encounter entities that are not welcome in your life.

Maybe you live somewhere that feels haunted, or you feel that someone may have put some kind of curse on you. This chapter also shows you how to counter these effects so that you can make your environment a safe and cozy one.

BELOW Psychic powers can be enhanced by using divination methods such as a crystal ball, or by using visualization techniques.

MEET YOUR SPIRIT GUIDE

A meditation to help you to meet your invisible helper

ALL OF US HAVE A SPIRIT GUIDE AND HAVE DONE SO SINCE THE DAY WE WERE BORN. THEY ARE BEINGS THAT WE CHOSE TO GIVE US HELP AND GUIDANCE ON EARTH WHILE WE WERE STILL ON THE OTHER SIDE, BEFORE BEING CONCEIVED IN OUR MOTHER'S WOMB. SPIRIT GUIDES ARE NOT NECESSARILY ANGELS, ALTHOUGH YOU MAY HAVE AN ANGEL HELPING YOU AT TIMES AS WELL, BUT ARE SPIRITUAL BEINGS DEDICATED TO YOUR DEVELOPMENT IN YOUR PRESENT LIFETIME.

Most people will be unaware of the help their spirit guide gives but will instead put their help down to a lucky dream, coincidence, instinct, or a hunch. How many times have you had a certain feeling about a person and have then been proved right? You can be certain that your spirit guide, on a subconscious level, has been at your side. Other people, who may have developed their psychic powers to a higher state, will actually be able to hear or even see their guides and may even be able to work with them to help others. Mediums and psychics (reputable ones, that is) are a good example of this.

If you wish to meet your spirit guide, be warned that it may take much meditation practice and a conscious desire to improve your psychic abilities. This will mean a daily practice of sitting quietly in a room with a candle and incense lit and following appropriate meditations or guided visualizations such as this one.

Quietly drift into a deeply relaxed state and visualize yourself in a natural setting that is familiar and special— one that feels safe to you. This may be a garden or a wood or a place by the sea, real or imaginary. Really feel the place, smell, touch, hear, and see it. Then sit down quietly and wait. When you are ready you may see a blue light

approaching you from the distance. This will come closer and closer until it takes on the form of a person. If he or she comes close enough, invite him or her to sit with you and talk. Ask their name and discuss whatever problems you have at present. When you are done, ask him or her if he or she will meet you there again when you next need to see him or her.

Conversely, instead of seeing your guide you may just hear his or her voice for now. Usually, this is over your right shoulder, but do not worry if it is different. Always be aware, though, that a true guide will never tell you to do things that would harm you or others. Once your guide has left you, slowly come back from your special place and out of the meditation. You may not be successful first time, but don't worry. These things, when done properly, happen when they are meant to and not before.

TAKE ...

A QUIET ROOM

A WHITE CANDLE

INCENSE OF YOUR CHOICE

A MAGICAL MINI HERB GARDEN

Plant special herbs for luck and harmony in the home

GARDENS ARE SPECIAL PLACES WITH A MAGIC OF THEIR OWN. BESIDES ATTRACTING NATURE SPIRITS, PLANTS ALSO CONTAIN OTHER PROPERTIES. THESE CAN BE MEDICINAL, CULINARY, OR MAGICAL; AND THUS CAN BE USED FOR MANY THINGS. PLANT YOUR OWN MINI GARDEN USING EITHER THE PLANTS LISTED OR OTHER ONES OF YOUR OWN CHOOSING. THIS GARDEN CONTAINS HERBS THAT WILL PROTECT THE HOME AND EXTEND THE BLESSINGS OF HEALTH, LUCK, HARMONY, AND PROSPERITY TO ALL WHO LIVE THERE.

You could start the garden from seed but it is easier and quicker to buy small, specially grown plants from your local nursery. Start by drawing a small pentacle on each of the crocks. Using this ancient symbol will give your plants an extra magical power. Place the crocks in the bottom of the pot and fill the pot with compost, almost to the brim. Make sure that your plants are well watered before you tap them out of their pots, and then gently make holes in the compost to lower them in. Firm the soil carefully around the roots and make sure that the rootball is just below the level of the soil. The plants for this spell were picked for the following properties:

Sage: harmony within the house, wisdom, and skill
Rosemary: good luck, remembrance of the ancestors
Basil: prosperity and protection
Thyme: health and strength

TAKE ...

A POT

SOME COMPOST

A FEW PIECES OF BROKEN CROCKS

SMALL HERB PLANTS OF:

SAGE

ROSEMARY

BASIL

THYME

A BIT OF GLITTER OF
STAR-SHAPED
SEQUINS

When you have finished planting,
give the compost a good watering, then
sprinkle the surface with a little glitter to
remind you how wonderful these plants
are. If you wish, you could say a
little prayer asking the plant spirits
to be healthy and strong. Place the
pot in a warm and sunny place
and remember to water it when
the soil is dry. If the rosemary
and sage get too large, they can
always be planted somewhere
outside or given away to a friend.

FAERY SHAKE

Shake up this Faery potion to awaken your inner child and bring laughter into your life

ALL SPIRITS LIKE THE SOUND OF MUSIC, ESPECIALLY RATTLES. FAERIES ARE NO EXCEPTION. HERE IS A RATTLE OR SHAKING STICK YOU CAN MAKE AT HOME JUST FOR THE LITTLE FOLK. IT IS BASED ON A RAIN STICK AS USED BY THE NATIVE AMERICANS, BUT, INSTEAD OF BRINGING A DOWNPOUR, IT SHOULD ATTRACT THE FAERY FOLK INTO YOUR LIFE, TOGETHER WITH THE FEELING OF JOY THEY BRING.

Take the cardboard tube and hammer in the nails at regular intervals up and down its length. Place one of the ends on the tube and fix it in place with either glue or some sticky tape. Next fill the tube with the rattling items. Faeries traditionally like fun things, so try to include as great a variety of things that make you smile. Once you have about the equivalent of a cup or two in the tube, tightly attach the other plastic end with glue or tape. To keep the nails safely in the tube, brush glue over the cardboard and wind the strips of material around until the whole tube is covered from top to bottom.

When you wish to call the spirits of fun into your life, slowly tilt the Faery shaker so that the rattling bits can fall through the nails. Then say:

Faeries, Faeries come and play;
Send my weary thoughts away.
Faery rattle Faeries call—
Laughter, fun, and love to all.

Next start hopping around the room, first on one leg, then the other, still rattling and chanting. Do this clockwise in a circle until you become breathless and dizzy. Then, immediately sit down quietly and hear the small tinkles of laughter around you.

TAKE ...

*A SMALL CARDBOARD TUBE WITH
TWO END PIECES*

*ONE POUND (450 GRAMS) OF
SMALL, FLAT-HEADED
NAILS (THE SAME LENGTH AS
THE TUBE'S DIAMETER)*

A HAMMER

GLUE

*STRIPS OF MATERIAL
(VELVET LOOKS AND
FEELS GOOD)*

A HANDFUL OF DRIED APPLE SEEDS

A HANDFUL OF SMALL POLISHED CRYSTALS

A FEW ROSEHIPS

*ANYTHING ELSE THAT RATTLES
THAT YOU FEEL WOULD
BE APPROPRIATE*

PSYCHIC SCRYING BOWL

A spell for harnessing the power of the moon

SCRYING IS THE ANCIENT ART OF LOOKING INTO THE
FUTURE OR OBTAINING ANSWERS FROM THE SPIRIT WORLD.
DEVELOP YOUR SCRYING POWERS WITH THE AID OF THIS
MAGICAL BOWL. THE HERB MUGWORT HAS ALWAYS BEEN
USED BY WITCHES TO PROMOTE SECOND SIGHT.

Make up the infusion of mugwort by adding a handful of the herb to a bowl of
boiling water and allow it to steep for ten minutes. Let the mixture cool and
strain the liquid off into a bottle. On the night of the full moon, take the glass bowl
outside and rub the inside of it with the infusion. Say:

> *Lady goddess of the moon, lend your power unto this bowl that it may
> aid me in the art of scrying.*

Keep the bowl outside all night, where it can absorb the moon's powers. Make sure,
though, that you rise before dawn to retrieve it before sunlight can touch it. Wrap
the bowl in the black silk cloth and keep it in a dark cupboard
for a month. This will let the essence of the mugwort
and the moonlight infuse themselves into
the material of the glass.
At the next full moon fill the bowl
with water and add a couple of drops of
the ink. Then take the bowl outside and place it
where the moon's reflection can just be seen in the
water. Pass your hand three times above the bowl and say:

> *Inky blackness and moon's secret power,
> Show me what I wish to know at this hour.*

Sit quietly and focus your eyes upon the water. At
first, stare at the image of the moon,
and then, as you feel yourself

becoming more relaxed, try to
focus beyond it. This is a
hard skill to master but
with practice it can be
done. After a while you
may find that the water
begins to swirl and
images or symbols will
appear before you.

After each scrying,
always clean your bowl
with the mugwort
infusion and keep it
wrapped in the black
cloth in a cupboard.

TAKE ...

A DARK GLASS BOWL

WATER

SOME BLACK INK

*A PIECE OF BLACK SILK
CLOTH*

*AN INFUSION OF
MUGWORT*

GHOSTBUSTER

Cleanse your home of any unwanted spiritual energies

SOMETIMES YOU MAY GET VISITORS TO YOUR
HOUSE WHO LEAVE BEHIND THEM UNWANTED
NEGATIVE SPIRITUAL ENERGIES. OR MAYBE
YOUR MAGICAL WORK HAS INADVERTENTLY
ATTRACTED UNWANTED GHOSTLY GUESTS WHO HAVE
DECIDED THAT YOUR PLACE IS INDEED A DESIRABLE
RESIDENCE. DON'T PANIC. THERE IS A GOOD WAY OF
BIDDING THESE ENERGIES GOOD-BYE, AND IT WILL MAKE
YOUR HOUSE SMELL NICE INTO THE BARGAIN.

Take your sweetgrass or sage and light it so that it is smoldering. Both of these
herbs are traditionally used in many Native American traditions to cleanse a
space or person in a ceremony called "smudging." Place the herb in your incense
dish so that you can carry it around. A small note about the dish here: Make sure
that it doesn't conduct heat too easily or else you may find it too hot to handle after
a while. I personally use a large paua or abalone shell, which does the job wonderfully.

Start by smudging yourself. Waft the smoke with the feather over your body
from head to toe, visualizing it cleaning your aura like a psychic shower. Then
walk around the room waving the smoke into every corner, nook, and cranny.
With each room say the words:

Be gone, all energies that are not welcome here.
You are banished from this room and from this house.

Imagine a dark cloud gathering near the center, which, with one last flick of the feather, spirals out of the window and back to wherever it came from. Cleanse every room of the house in this manner—don't forget ones that are rarely used, such as a basement or attic. When you have finished, find a quiet place to sit and meditate. Feel your heart fill with the golden glow of unconditional love for the place in which you live. Then let this beautiful energy flow through you and fill the entire house.

TAKE ...

AN INCENSE DISH

SWEETGRASS BRAID OR SAGE (NATIVE AMERICAN VARIETY)

A LARGE FEATHER

HUDU DOLL

This Brazilian healing charm will banish bad luck for good

HUDU OR VOODOO DOLLS COME FROM THE VODOUN TRADITION OF THE CARIBBEAN. THE BASICS OF THIS RELIGION FIRST ARRIVED FROM AFRICA WITH THE SLAVE TRADE, BUT IT STILL THRIVES TODAY. MENTION THE WORD "VOODOO" AND MOST PEOPLE IMMEDIATELY THINK OF ZOMBIES AND DOLLS WITH PINS STICKING IN THEM. WHILE THESE CONCEPTS ARE A SMALL PART OF THE TRADITION, VOODOO MAGIC IS MOSTLY USED TO HELP RATHER THAN HARM.

Adapted from a Brazilian healing charm, this Voodoo doll is one of those that are designed to help, not harm. It will watch over you and banish any jinx or bad luck you feel might be hanging around.

Take the two twig sticks and tie them into a cross shape. This will form the basis for the body. Next, tie moss over the sticks to build up the body shape. While you are doing this, start to hum. Let the hum form itself into any tune you like, for this is the song that brings the doll into being. Next sew material onto the doll in the shape of a face and clothes, arms, and legs. It doesn't have to look perfect—it will create itself the way it wants to be. That is the beauty of this kind of magic. Sew on eyes and a smiling mouth and then attach your decorations to its clothing.

When your doll is made, tap it lightly three times: on the forehead, over the heart, and over the stomach. Say:

Wake up, wake up, wake up. I give you the name Luck Doll and ask that you send away all bad luck and jinxes. Instead, fill my life with happiness, health, and wealth.

Spend some time focusing on things you want in your life before hanging the doll above the doorway of your house.

TAKE ...

2 SMALL BUT STRONG TWIGS

STRING

MOSS

*DIFFERENT-COLORED PIECES
   OF MATERIAL*

*DECORATIONS YOU FEEL RELEVANT (FOR
   EXAMPLE, BUTTONS, FEATHERS, BRAID)*

NEEDLE AND THREAD

HEALING CRYSTAL SPELL

Let illness flow from your body with this crystal spell

ALL STONES AND CRYSTALS HAVE AMAZING POWERS
OF RECEPTIVITY. CRYSTALS IN PARTICULAR HAVE THE
ABILITY TO TAKE ON WHATEVER YOU ASK OF THEM,
WHICH MAKES THEM PARTICULARLY GOOD FOR HEALING
PURPOSES. ALWAYS REMEMBER, THOUGH, TO TREAT
YOUR CRYSTAL WITH RESPECT.

Light the candle and sit quietly, holding the crystal. Feel it getting warmer in
your hand as it tunes in to your energy. Speak to it quietly and tell it about
your illness and the way it makes you feel. Ask it to absorb the sickness from your
body and promise it that it will be cleansed afterward. Again, sit quietly until you
"feel" that the crystal has accepted your request.

Stand up and slowly begin to rub the crystal over your whole body, especially at
the site of sickness. As you do this, visualize the illness leaving your body: maybe
see it in the form of little black worms. As it leaves you, the illness enters into the
crystal and disappears.

Once you have completed this, take the crystal and immediately place it in a
glass of water. Add the salt and say:

Crystal be cleansed,
Crystal be bright,
All illness leave—
By this rite,
Flow away
Far from me.
As I do will,
So mote it be.

Leave the crystal in
the water for a few
hours while you go
and splash yourself
with cold water. Dry off
and go and rest. To complete
the cleansing of the crystal,
carefully pour the water in the glass
down the sink. Rinse the glass and the
crystal with fresh water, and then leave
them somewhere in the open air—
preferably in the sun—to dry. The
sunshine will also reenergize the crystal,
since this exercise will have left its
natural energies a little depleted.

TAKE ...

A QUARTZ CRYSTAL

A WHITE CANDLE

A GLASS OF WATER

SALT

BEWITCHING
SEASONS

CELEBRATE THE WHEEL OF THE YEAR

WITCHES HAVE THEIR OWN CALENDAR TO CELEBRATE THE TURNING WHEEL OF THE YEAR. EACH FESTIVAL RECOGNIZES IMPORTANT ELEMENTS OF DIFFERENT PARTS OF THE YEAR AND IS OFTEN ACCOMPANIED BY AN APPROPRIATE RITUAL.

WINTER SOLSTICE/ YULE
DECEMBER 21

Celebration of the rebirth of the sun

IMBOLC
FEBRUARY 2

Celebration of the goddess after giving birth to the sun; a festival of light, warmth, and hope for the year to come

SPRING EQUINOX
MARCH 21

Celebration of the beginning of spring

BELTANE
APRIL 30

Celebration of fertility and inspiration

However, as this is a book about spellcraft rather than witchcraft, it would not be right to go into detail about the ceremonies involved—other books cover that subject matter more than adequately. Instead, here is a brief summary of the festivals and their approximate dates, just in case you wish to celebrate in your own way at that time.

For those who wish to mark the seasons differently, this chapter includes seasonal spells that capture the essence and energy of the time of year. Use them and adapt them to your needs and you will still find a great satisfaction in weaving your magic through the spokes of the wheel of the year. Also in this chapter are some extra-special spells that are sealed and are therefore to be used only when they are really, really needed.

Happy spelling!

SUMMER SOLSTICE
JUNE 21

Celebration of the sun at his strongest; the longest day

LUGHNASADH
AUGUST 1

Celebration of the first of the harvest; the wane of the sun god's reign

AUTUMN EQUINOX
SEPTEMBER 21

Celebration of the culmination of the harvest; a time of reflection over the past year

SAMHAIN
OCTOBER 31

Celebration of the ancestors, when the veil between the worlds is thinnest; the Celtic New Year

ORACLE OF SPRING

A spell for renewal and "spring cleaning" the soul, mind, and body

WITH SPRING COMES A FEELING OF RENEWAL, A FEELING THAT ALL THINGS ARE POSSIBLE. IT IS TIME FOR A NEW START, TIME TO THROW OFF THE QUIETNESS OF WINTER AND BEGIN PUTTING INTO MOTION ALL THOSE PROJECTS YOU'VE BEEN DREAMING ABOUT. HOWEVER, IF YOU HAVE DIFFICULTY CHOOSING WHICH ONE TO START FIRST, USE THIS SIMPLE SPRING ORACLE TO HELP YOU CHOOSE.

Take three beans (such as kidney beans) and decide which one will represent which project. Pick up the pot of compost and stir the soil clockwise three times with your left index finger while saying:

Finger of fate, point the way;
Oracle lead me not astray;
The seed so strong and fast to grow,
Will point the way, my path to show.

Then plant the beans in the soil. With each one, strongly focus on what it is you wish to achieve. Add a little plant marker beside each one so you know what each bean represents to you. Water the soil and place a little plastic bag over the top to retain the humidity. At this point take a little quiet time and utter a small prayer, asking the powers that be to direct you wisely and give you the confidence and strength needed to find the success you require in the coming year.

Place the pot in a warm place, such as a cupboard or a sunny windowsill, for a few days. Check every day for sprouts pushing through the soil. When you see one, check the marker and you will have the answer as to which project you should concentrate on first. Take the plastic bag off the pot and place the pot in a warm, light place. Keep an eye on what happens to all the plants, since this is part of the oracle. When they are strong enough and the danger of frost has passed, you may plant them outside and continue to nurture your dreams.

TAKE ...

BEANS

A POT OF COMPOST

MARKER STICKS

SUMMER WORSHIP

*Awaken from your winter slumber
and celebrate the energy of the sun*

THE PURPOSE IS TO CAPTURE THE ESSENCE OF
SUMMER AND SAVE IT SO THAT ITS MAGIC
WILL CHEER YOU ON RAINY DAYS. PICK A
WARM SUMMER'S DAY. IF YOU CAN DO THIS
SPELL AT SUMMER SOLSTICE (JUNE 21), ALL
THE BETTER, BECAUSE THIS IS WHEN SUMMER
IS AT ITS HEIGHT.

First, find a sunny spot outside. Raise your arms to the
sun and say:

*God of the sun, all Father, who is known by many names
such as Apollo, Lugh, Ra, and Sol, may your blessing fall
on whatsoever your rays touch. May all the flowers and trees
be filled with your bright essence. Bless also my footsteps that
they take me to whatever I shall need for this spell.*

Sit down for a few minutes and focus on what essence of summer
you would like to capture. Then get up and go for a walk. Let your
mind drift and be aware of anything that catches your eye. This could
be a flower, a leaf, a feather—anything. If, as you look at it, it speaks
to you of summer, take it with you. If this means picking a flower or a
leaf, leave behind a small token of thanks such as a
piece of hair or a pinch of tobacco.
Continue collecting
for an hour.

TAKE ...

A FLOWER PRESS

A CARD

GLUE

Upon returning to the house, take the flowers and leaves and dry them in a flower press. This could take a few weeks. Put the remainder of the items aside in a safe place. When the flowers are pressed, gather the whole of your collection together with the card and glue. Cut the card in a circle and arrange the items over it in a colorful montage or mandala. Once it is finished, hold your hands over it and say:

Essence of summer, you are charmed to keep your warmth and brightness and take me through the long dark days that lie ahead. All this I charge in the name of the Earth Mother and the Father Sun. So mote it be.

Hang the picture up somewhere prominent; then, when you need some cheering up or warmth, put your hand upon it and visualize the warmth and brightness of your walk.

Sealed Spell

ETERNAL ENERGY

An interactive spell that, when opened for the first time, will empower you with eternal magical energy

ONCE YOU HAVE PERFORMED THIS SPELL YOU WILL HAVE UNLOCKED A METHOD THAT WILL PROVIDE YOU WITH ALL THE MAGICAL ENERGY YOU'LL EVER NEED. THE SYMBOLS—A PENTAGRAM REPRESENTING MAGIC, AND THE SIGN OF INFINITY—ARE DESIGNED TO ALIGN YOUR MIND TO YOUR OWN INNER POTENTIAL. THE ENERGY CHARGE AFFIRMS THIS POTENTIAL AND PROVIDES YOU WITH THE KNOWLEDGE THAT YOU ARE INFINITELY UNIQUE AND MAGICAL IN YOUR OWN RIGHT.

To start the spell, let your finger rest on the top point of the pentagram. From then on, follow the lines of the pentagram, proceeding from the top to the bottom left point, all the while reciting the Energy Charge.

THE ENERGY CHARGE

I am the wind that whispers in the trees. I am the sun that creates both garden and desert. I am the wide-ranging ocean and all the fish that swim within. I am the deep caverns, the womb of the earth within which all mysteries are treasured. I am the dancing fire, the whirling tornado, and the eagle's cry. I am the infinite spirit, which never dies. I am the serenity of the moon and the council of the stars. I am a child created from stardust and the very magic of the cosmos itself. I am the universe and it is I. I am unique within this world and I affirm that within the love that lies within my heart, all things are possible. Therefore I claim my birthright of inner power and inner love that will always grant me the energy I need.

TAKE ...

JUST THE SPELL
ON THIS PAGE

When you have
finished reading
this, take three
deep breaths,
breathing in the
magic around you, the magic that connects
you to everything else. This spell may be used to
give you an energy reboost from time to time if needed.

FALL MAGIC

A very witchy ritual to align with the shape-shifting energies of fall

FALL IS THE TIME OF YEAR WHEN WE ARE CELEBRATING THE BRINGING IN OF THE HARVEST AND MOURNING THE PASSING OF SUMMER. THEREFORE, IT CAN BE SEEN AS BOTH A TIME OF GARNERING IN WHAT WE HAVE SOWN THROUGHOUT THE YEAR AND OF LETTING GO OF ANYTHING THAT IS HOLDING US BACK. AS HARVEST TIME IS A CELEBRATION, WHY NOT THROW A PARTY AFTER THE RITUAL?

Sit by the fire with six nuts beside you. Start with a nut that represents something you have achieved during the year. Maybe you passed an examination or you got the job you wanted. All you need to say is:

> *This nut represents the _____ that I have harvested this year.*

Put the nut in your velvet bag. The next nut should represent something you wish to let go of, maybe a trait in your personality you don't like, or an irrational fear. Say:

> *This nut represents the _____ that I wish to let go of.*

Hurl the nut into the flames and watch it burn, all the while

visualizing whatever it was disappearing from your life. Carry on like this alternately for the other four nuts until three of the nuts are safely garnered in your pouch and the other three have been burned to ash. Next, bless the food. Hold out your arms to encompass all before you and say:

Ancient gods and goddesses of this land, good spirits and ancestors, I thank you for this food and for all you have given me throughout the year. I ask that you sustain my spirit through the dark months and that you give your love and protection over me, my family, and my friends. Bless this food that all who partake shall be healthy, wealthy, and wise.

At this point, hopefully, your guests will start arriving and the party can begin!

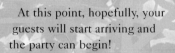

TAKE ...

AN OPEN FIRE OR BONFIRE

A LITTLE BROWN VELVET BAG

HAZELNUTS

A HARVEST FEAST TO INCLUDE APPLES, PUMPKINS, AND SQUASH, BREAD, NUTS, BERRIES, BEER, CIDER, AND MEAD

Sealed Spell

SOUL MATE CHARM

Use only when you are ready to attract your one true love—for it can never be used again!

THIS IS A SPELL TO HELP YOU FIND THAT LOVE OF YOUR LIFE, WHEREVER THAT PERSON MAY BE. BUT BE WARNED: THIS SPELL CAN BE USED ONLY ONCE, SO MAKE SURE THAT THE TIME IS RIGHT FOR YOU.

On the night of the new moon, light the candles on your altar and also some incense if you wish. Take the two pieces of copper, a metal sacred to Venus, the goddess of love, and begin to twist them together while repeating:

Me to he,
He to me,
Brought together
Our hearts shall be.
I to he,
He to me,
Our lives entwined,
I will it to be.
Across the miles,
Across this space,
Let me know my
beloved's face.

Finish the copper twist by bending it into a circle so that the ends meet. Then place it in your pouch along with the rose petals and the piece of your hair. Now it is time to affirm your intentions

on the psychic plane. Sit quietly and visualize yourself walking to the top of a hill. From the top you can see forever, or so it seems. Turning to your right, you notice an unlit beacon of dried wood. Concentrating hard, you magically produce a golden flame from the tip of your finger and touch it to the wood. The wood ignites at once, sending a flare of light into the sky. You touch the velvet pouch at your side (which you have carried with you into the visualization) and call out into the world beyond:

I am here, come to me. By all the powers of the universe, my soul mate, I bid you come.

Perform this visualization every night leading up to the full moon and carry your soul mate charm with you at all times.

TAKE ...

2 PINK CANDLES

2 PIECES OF COPPER WIRE

A PINK OR WHITE VELVET POUCH

DRIED ROSE PETALS

A PIECE OF YOUR HAIR

WINTER WEAVING

A charm to protect and warm the home and hearth, and to align with the spirit of Yule

WINTER IS A TIME OF QUIET REFLECTION AND HOPEFUL DREAMS OF WHAT WILL BE IN THE COMING YEAR. THE CULMINATION OF THIS SEASON IS THE FESTIVAL OF YULE (DECEMBER 21), WHEN THE SUN IS REBORN AND THE DAYS BEGIN TO GET LONGER AGAIN. IT IS A TIME OF THINKING ABOUT DEATH AND REBIRTH. IT IS ALSO A TIME FOR THINKING OF THE FAMILY AND THE HOME.

Take the three twigs and spray them with the gold or silver spray paint. If you wish, you may also add some glitter to make them twinkle. When they are dry, arrange them in a star pattern and tie them firmly at the center. Next, take one of the threads and begin to wind it in and out of the frame of sticks, with each successive pass tight against the previous one. As you weave the threads, hum a tune, any tune that you find restful. You may even find that you don't even recognize it—that it has come out of thin air! As you weave and hum, visualize a large protective web, made from golden-spun light, being woven over your home. Once it is finished, hold it high in the air to each of the four directions—north, south, east, and west, and at each one declare:

Powers of the _____[direction], I call upon you to witness this charm and protect my home and family.

Finally, take the decorations and attach them, one by one, to the charm. With each attachment, state its purpose. For example, you may have a small heart-shaped bauble. When you affix it, you could say:

This is for [name of person]. May he/she find all the love he/she needs in the coming year.

TAKE ...

*3 STRONG TWIGS, APPROXIMATELY 9
INCHES (22 CENTIMETERS) IN LENGTH*

SOME SILVER OR GOLD SPRAY PAINT

GLITTER (OPTIONAL)

GOLD, SILVER, AND GLITTERY RED THREAD

*SMALL BAUBLES, BEADS, OR OTHER SYMBOLIC
YULE DECORATIONS*

Other decorations could include feathers, crystals, paper
beads, and so on. But try not to overload the charm—
and the magic. Finally, hang it somewhere prominent.

Sealed Spell

ULTIMATE BANISHER

A spell to eject from your life someone you do not want to see again—without causing them harm!

TAKE ...

A STICK OF CHARCOAL

A BLACK CANDLE

A SMALL PIECE OF PAPER

THERE MAY BE SOMEONE IN YOUR LIFE—MAYBE A VICIOUS GOSSIP OR A NASTY EX-BOYFRIEND—WHO CASTS A LONG SHADOW OVER YOUR EVERY WAKING MOMENT. THIS SPELL IS DESIGNED TO BANISH THEM FROM YOUR LIFE FOR GOOD BUT WITHOUT CAUSING THEM HARM, WHICH WOULD REFLECT BADLY ON YOUR OWN KARMA.

During a waning moon on a Saturday, write the name of the person to be banished in charcoal on the piece of paper. As you write, visualize the person and the things he or she has done to upset you. Draw a circle around the name and say:

So are you enclosed, _____ [name of person].
I catch you and keep you within this boundary of black,
That you may hear my words this night.
With this spell I cast you from my life's circle;
I throw you where you cannot touch my light.
From this moment you shall trouble me no more.
By the names of all the high gods
And the angels of the cosmos,
By this great magic you are gone—
Without harm,
Without malice,
And with only a blessing that you
*   become a better person.*
So mote it be.

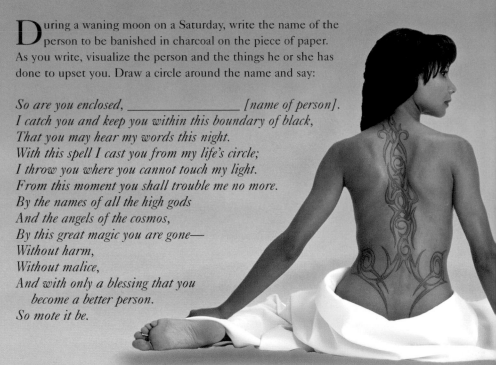

Carefully burn the piece of paper
in the flame of the candle. Do this
in a fire grate, outdoors, or in the sink,
where there is no danger of setting
fire to anything. Collect the ash in
a little dish and divide it into three.
Take one-third of the ash and bury
it in the ground saying:

*So my worries are buried deep and
 shall not surface again.*

Take the next third and throw it into some
flowing water. Say as you do so:

*So my fears flow from me this day and shall
 never return.*

Finally, take the remaining ash to a high
place and cast it to the wind. Say:

*All that torments me shall be taken on the
 wind far from me. And so I am free.*

INDEX

A

abundance 36
achievement, to celebrate 118
air (element) 14, 15, 52, 69
altar 8, 46, 66, 70
angels 94
Aphrodite 60
assignments, for help with 20–21
aura 32–33
   to cleanse 102

B

banishment, spell of 124–125
Bath Fizzler 62–63
bath oil 84–85
beauty: inner 75, 86–87
   spells for 78–79, 84–85
Bright Eyes 88–89
broken heart, to heal 68–69

C

candles 8, 15
   colors of 8
   spells using 29, 38, 44, 46, 52, 66, 68, 70, 94, 106, 120
Career Chooser 50–51
chakras 76–77
choosing: a career 50–51
   a project 112–113
City Oasis 26–27
clary sage 86
cleansing rituals 30–31, 102–103
Cleopatra's Oil 84–85
colors: of chakras 77
   meanings of 8, 38

competitions, for luck in 48
Computer Charmer 24–25
confidence, to increase 28–29, 53, 87
Crowning Glory 82–83
crystals 8, 88, 106–107
   to cleanse 106
   to reenergize 107

D

days of the week 12, 13
   see also Friday; Monday; Saturday
destroying a spell 10
dew 79

E

earth (element) 14
   spells using 39, 50, 52, 60, 64, 69
Easy Essays 20–21
elements 14–15, 52, 69, 125
   see also air; earth; fire; water
energy: absorption of 64
   elemental 14–15
   lunar 58
   magical 9, 10, 116
   negative 30, 102–103
   planetary 13
   sun's 12, 41
   universal 76
Energy Charge 116
environment, to protect 12, 30–31, 93
essential oils 26, 62–63
Eternal Energy 116–117

exam nerves, to overcome 38–39
eyes, to refresh 88–89

F

Face Magic 78–79
Faery Shake 98–99
Fall Magic 118–119
family, to protect 122–123
feathers 8, 50, 102–103
festivals 110–111
Fidelity Knot 70–71
fire (element) 15, 15, 52, 69
flowers 78, 88, 114–115
focus 8, 9, 10
Forever Friends 22–23
Friday, spells for 22–23, 66–67
friendship: to create 28–29
   to repair 22–23
full moon 12, 58, 70, 100, 121
future, to decide 50–51

G

Ghostbuster 102–103
goddess 12
goddesses, warrior 33

H

hair potion 82–83
harmony, to restore 22–23, 64–65
harvest 111, 118
healing 15, 106–107
Healing Crystal Spell 106–107
herb garden 96
herbs 20, 30, 42, 82–83, 86, 96–97, 102

home, to protect 96, 122–123
homework, for help with
20–21
Hudu Doll 104–105

I

I Want You Back 66–67
illness, to banish 106–107
In with the In-Crowd 28–29
incense 8, 15
spells using 38, 52, 68,
94, 120
ingredient portfolio 19
inner beauty 75, 86–87
inner child, to awaken
98–99
inner eye 92
inner worlds 93

J

Jupiter 13, 38, 48, 49

K

Kiss Me Quick 58–59

L

letting go ritual 118–119
love: to encourage 60–61,
62–63
to rekindle 60–61, 66–67
Love Starter 60–61
luck 36, 48, 49
bad, to banish 104–105
Luck, Be a Lady 48–49

M

Magical Mini Herb
Garden 96–97

mascot 52–53
meditation, guided 92–93,
94
Meet Your Spirit Guide
94–95
Merlin's Gold 40–41
Mirror, Mirror 86–87
Monday, spell for 46–47
money spells 14, 36, 42–43
Money Spinner 42–43
moon 12, 13
see also full moon; new
moon; waning moon
moonlight 12, 79
Mother Earth 76, 81, 83
mugwort 100–101
My Body, My Temple
76–77

N

Native American traditions
98, 102
nature spirits 96
negative magic 7
new moon 12, 46, 60, 66,
68, 120

O

opportunities, to create
40–41
Oracle of Spring 112–113

P

paganism/pagans 6, 12
pentagram/pentacle 14, 44,
96, 116
Perfect Saturday Job Spell
46–47

photographs, spells using
66–67, 70–71
plants 8
see also flowers; herbs
pollution, to counteract
30–31
problems, to banish 64–65
protection: of environment
12, 30–31
of home and family
96, 122–123
personal 32–33
psychic power 92, 94
Psychic Scrying Bowl
100–101

R

rattle, faery 98
Relationship Booster 64–65
relaxation, charm for 26–27
rosemary 30, 96, 97
rules of magic 10
runes 58

S

salt 30, 80, 106
Saturday, spell for 124
Saturday job, to obtain
46–47
scrying 100–101
sealed spells 116–117,
120–121, 124–125
seasons 8, 12–13, 110
second sight 100
secrecy 18–19, 23
seeds 40–41
shaking stick 98
shamans 6

Shop Till You Drop 44–45
shyness, to overcome 28–29
skin potion 78–79
Smog Buster 30–31
smudging 102
Soul-mate Charm 120–121
spirit guide 93, 94–95
Spot Be Gone 80–81
spring magic 112–113
stones 14
    spells using 40–41,
      50–51, 60–61, 64–65
summer solstice 111, 114
Summer Worship 114–115
sun 12, 13, 40–41, 107,
      111, 114
    square of 40
symbols 44, 116, 122

T
thanks offering 8, 83, 114
To Heal a Broken Heart
      68–69
Top of the Class 38–39
Tried and Tested 52–53

U
Ultimate Banisher 124–125
Urban Warrior 32–33

V
Venus 13, 22, 120
visualization 10, 26–27, 29,
      42, 53, 70, 76, 92–93,
      121, 122, 124
voodoo 104

W
waning moon 12, 124
warrior marks 32
water (element) 15
    spells using 52–53,
      65–66, 69–70, 106–107
will 7, 10, 92
Winter Weaving 122–123
witchcraft/witches 7, 8, 12,
      18, 74–75, 78, 86, 100, 110

Y
Yule 111, 122–123

CREDITS

t = top, b = bottom, l = left, r = right,
c = center, b/g = background

The Art Archive 74tl (Museo del Prado, Madrid/Dagli
Orti), 84tl (Musée des Beaux Arts, Antwerp/ Dagli Orti)
Fortean Picture Library 7r, 18tc, 98tr
Trip 12b/g (H. Rogers), 32bl

All other photographs and illustrations are the
copyright of Quarto. While every effort has
been made to credit contributors, we
apologize should there have been
any omissions or errors.